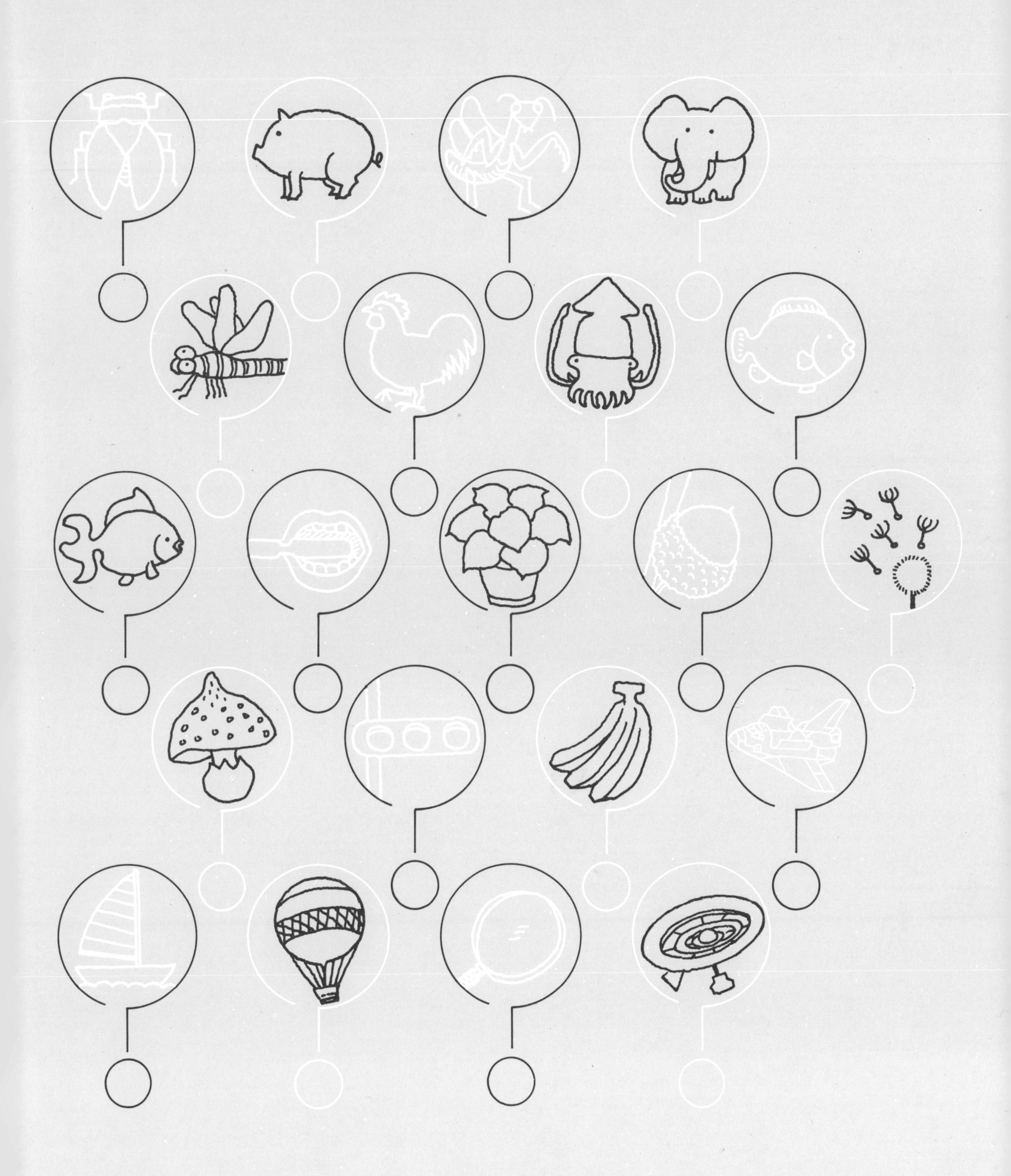

A Child's First Library of Learning

Science Starter

TIME LIFE ASIA

Contents

What Is It like inside Earth?

Earth is made up of three parts. They are the crust, the mantle and the core. The core is divided into the inner core and the outer core. The crust is on the outside and the core is in the centre. The mantle is between them.

Outer

Inner core

• To the Parent

Scientists have determined the composition of Earth's interior by studying seismic waves. Seismic waves are the vibrations that spread out from the focus of earthquakes. They have been recorded and their strengths measured when they reach Earth's surface. They have revealed that the lithosphere, which consists of plates that move as a result of convection currents in the mantle, is about 62 miles (100 km) thick; the mantle is 1,800 miles (2,900 km) thick. Estimates of the core's temperature range from 7,200° to 11,000° Fahrenheit (4,000° to 6,000°C.).

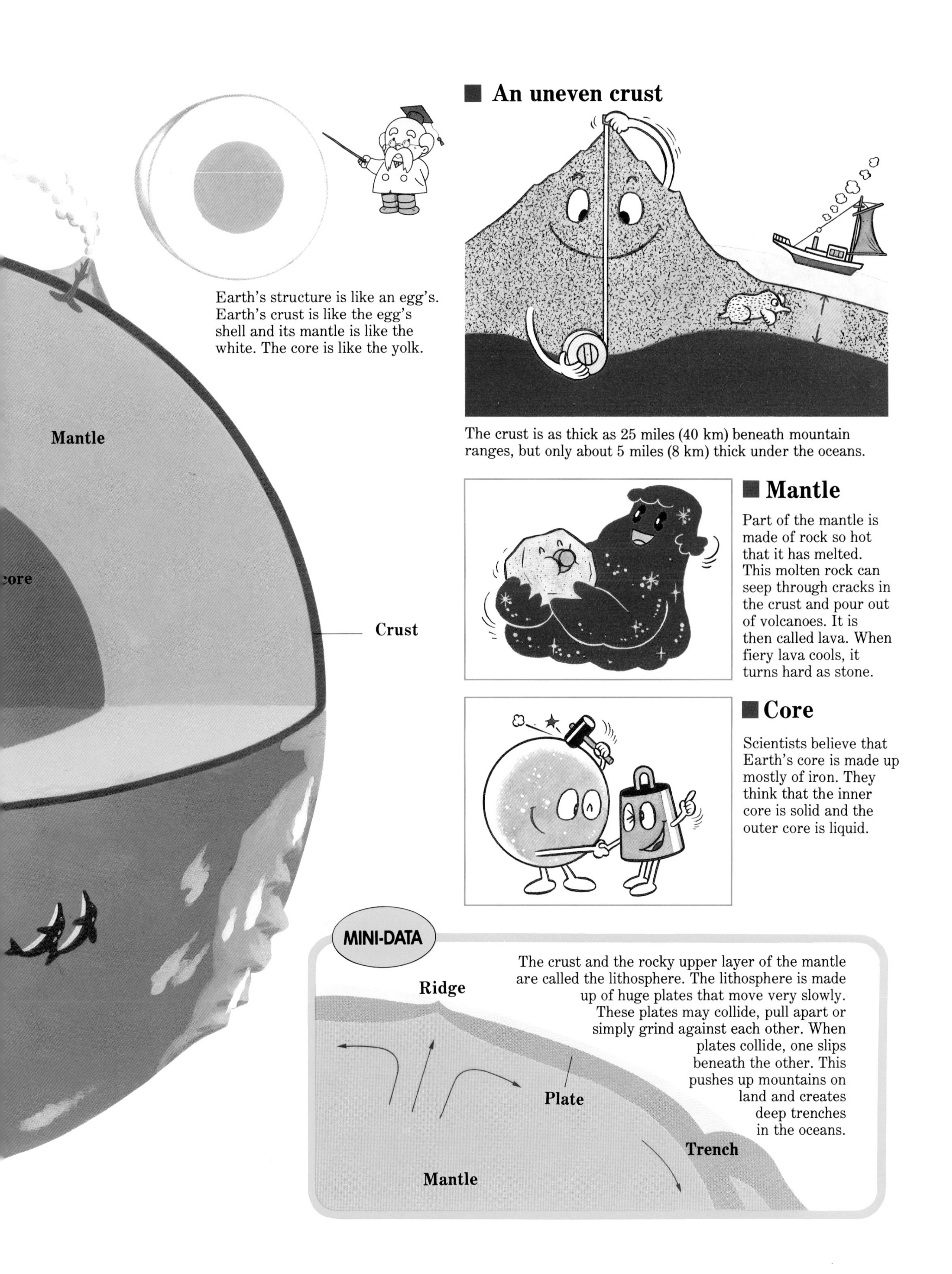

Earth's structure is like an egg's. Earth's crust is like the egg's shell and its mantle is like the white. The core is like the yolk.

An uneven crust

The crust is as thick as 25 miles (40 km) beneath mountain ranges, but only about 5 miles (8 km) thick under the oceans.

Mantle

Part of the mantle is made of rock so hot that it has melted. This molten rock can seep through cracks in the crust and pour out of volcanoes. It is then called lava. When fiery lava cools, it turns hard as stone.

Core

Scientists believe that Earth's core is made up mostly of iron. They think that the inner core is solid and the outer core is liquid.

MINI-DATA

The crust and the rocky upper layer of the mantle are called the lithosphere. The lithosphere is made up of huge plates that move very slowly. These plates may collide, pull apart or simply grind against each other. When plates collide, one slips beneath the other. This pushes up mountains on land and creates deep trenches in the oceans.

Why Does a Compass Point North?

ANSWER The inside of Earth acts like a strong magnet. One end of Earth's magnet is near the North Pole. The other end is near the South Pole. A compass has a needle that is a magnet. Earth's magnet attracts the needle so that it always points north.

The north and south poles of magnets attract each other.

How to use a compass

A compass needle always points north. Once you know which way north is you can figure out east, west and south

A ship's compass

Compasses have long been used on ships. They help captains get to where they want to go.

MINI-DATA

If you held a compass near the North Pole, the N of the compass would point straight to the ground.

• To the Parent

Most of the outer core of Earth is made of molten iron, which moves as a result of internal heat flows and Earth's rotation. This movement creates an electric current that makes the core a huge electromagnet. Earth, therefore, acts like a magnet whose ends lie near the North and South poles. Lines of magnetic force between these two ends curve around the planet. A compass needle will align itself with these lines.

What Kinds of Materials Are the Planets Made Of?

ANSWER As well as Earth there are eight other planets that circle, or orbit, the sun. Mercury, Venus, Earth and Mars are made mostly of rock. Jupiter, Saturn, Uranus and Neptune are made mostly of gases. Pluto, the most distant planet, is like an icy rock.

■ Pluto

As the farthest planet from the sun, it takes Pluto 248 years to circle the sun once. It is about one-fifth the size of Earth and is dark and cold with temperatures as low as -360° Fahrenheit (-220° C.). It is made of rocky material and ice, and has a covering of methane frost.

• To the Parent

As well as the nine planets, other bodies that orbit the sun include the planets' moons, countless asteroids and many comets. The sun and its satellites make up the Solar System, which is located about two-thirds from the centre of the Milky Way. This galaxy is just one of a cluster of 30 galaxies called the Local Group, which is one of many galaxy clusters that make up a supercluster.

How Is the Size of Earth Measured?

ANSWER We cannot find out Earth's size by using a tape measure. It is too big. Instead we have to use mathematics. One way is to look at a star from two places on Earth's surface. If we know the distance between those two places, we can figure out how big Earth is all the way round.

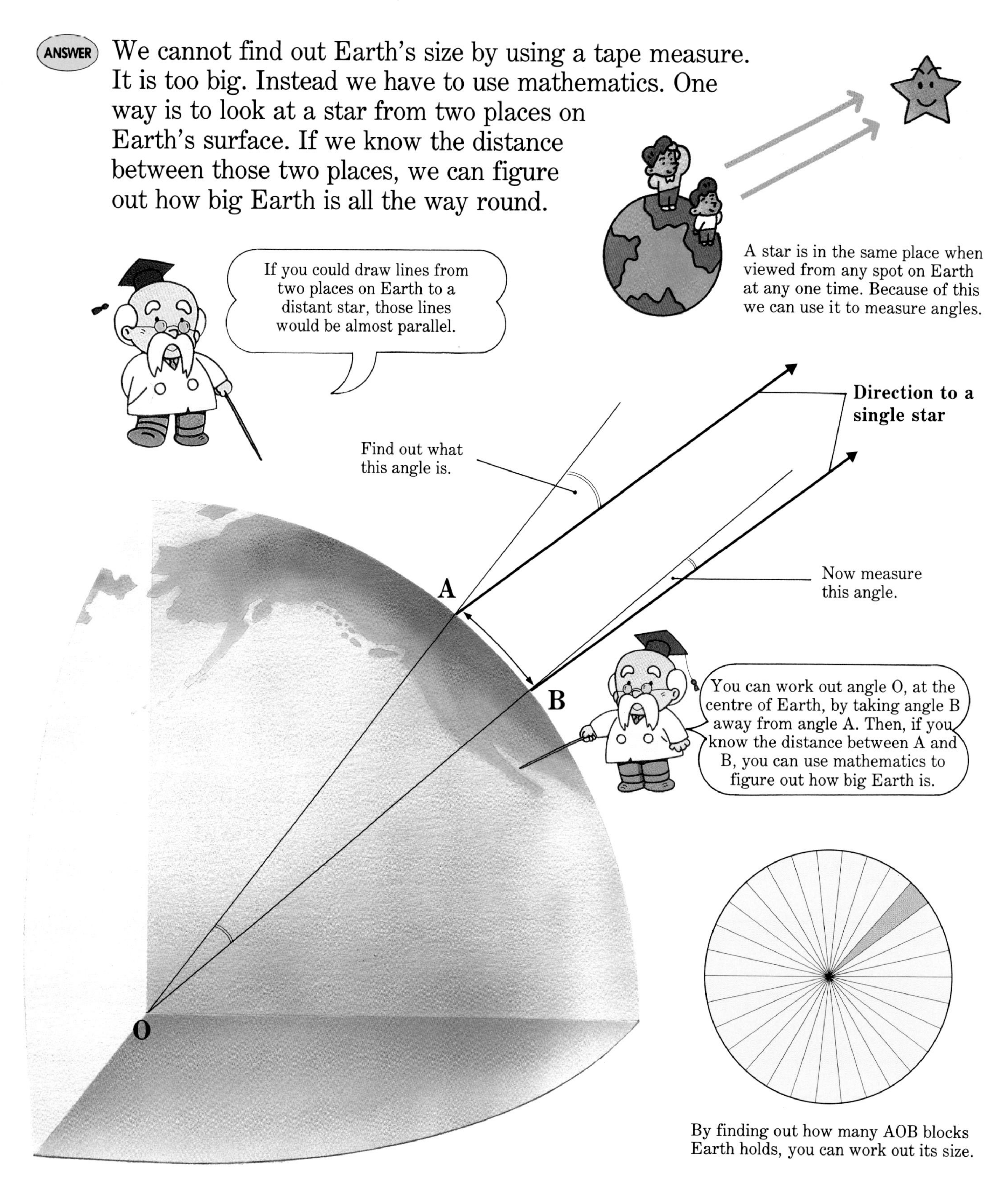

A star is in the same place when viewed from any spot on Earth at any one time. Because of this we can use it to measure angles.

By finding out how many AOB blocks Earth holds, you can work out its size.

Measuring Earth from a satellite

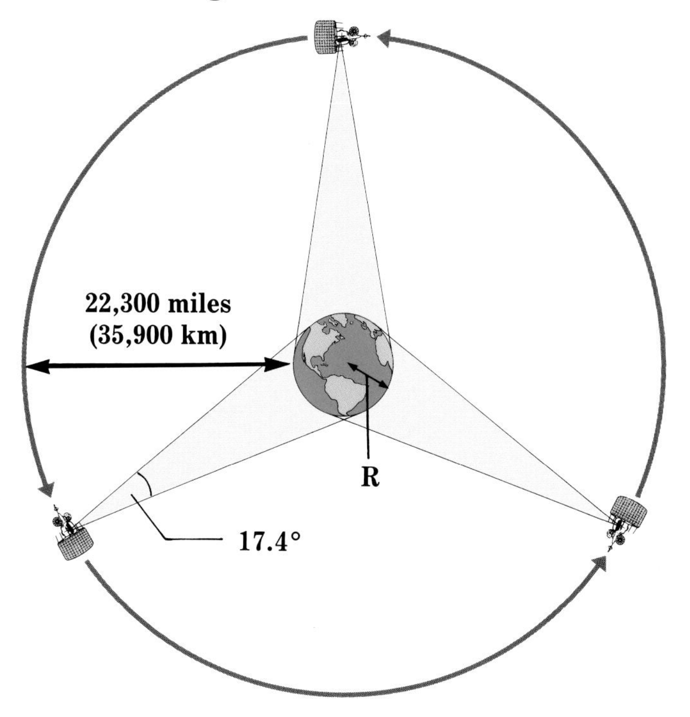

Another way to measure Earth is with the help of special satellites that are used for mapping. They observe Earth from 22,300 miles (35,900 km) in space. These satellites can measure the angle between themselves and two places on Earth. Once scientists know what one of these angles is, they can use it to figure out Earth's radius. That is the distance from the centre of Earth to its surface. If you know the radius of a circle, you can use mathematics to work out the length around the circle.

How an ancient Greek measured Earth

The Greek scholar Eratosthenes studied the shadow made by a tower in Alexandria, Egypt. He measured the angle that the shadow made at noon on the longest day of the year.

He knew that on the same day at the same time in Syene the sun was at its highest point. It shone straight down into a well, so it must be directly overhead.

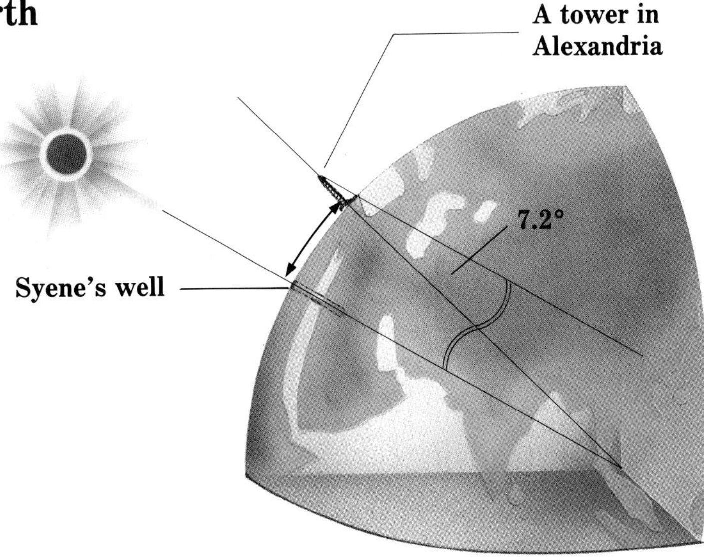

The angle Eratosthenes measured at Alexandria was 7.2°, or a fiftieth of a circle. So, he multiplied the distance between Syene and Alexandria by 50 to get the size of Earth. He found that it was about 25,000 miles (40,000 km) around.

• To the Parent

In the sixth century BC, Pythagoras reasoned that Earth is round because both the sun and moon are. But it was Eratosthenes in the third century BC who first used a scientific method to measure Earth's size. His estimate was very near the 24,902 miles (40,075 km) now known to be the circumference of the planet at the equator. Today's sophisticated equipment has shown that Earth is 26 miles (42 km) thicker at the equator than around the poles.

How Were the Oceans Made?

ANSWER The oceans were made when Earth was forming. Early on, Earth was very hot and gases escaped from it. Steam was also released and it covered the planet with thick clouds. As Earth cooled, rain fell from these clouds. Water collected in low-lying places on Earth's surface. As more and more rain fell, the water got deeper and formed oceans.

As Earth spun it got smaller. The heavier materials went to the centre and the lighter ones rose to the surface. Earth was so hot at first that the surface rocks were molten. Gases, including steam, bubbled out of this liquid rock. More gases and steam were forced out of Earth with lava from volcanoes. The steam formed huge clouds.

Many scientists think that the planets and the sun were formed from a large cloud of dust and gas. Sections of this cloud began to spin. In these places, dust and gas collected and stuck together. These spinning collections of dust and gas also attracted other matter. Over time these bodies grew into Earth, the other planets and the sun.

• To the Parent

Many scientists believe that eddies in a nebula—a cloud of dust and gas—condensed to form the Solar System. They think that Earth was once much bigger than it is now. As the planet spun, it shrank, causing inner temperatures to rise. Gravity pulled iron and other heavy metals to the core, while a thick mantle of molten rock covered the outside. Gases and water vapour rose from the liquid rock and lava flows to form a primitive atmosphere. The water vapour formed clouds. However, Earth was too hot for the rain from the clouds to settle and it simply vaporized to form clouds again. It was millions of years before Earth became cool enough for the rain to settle.

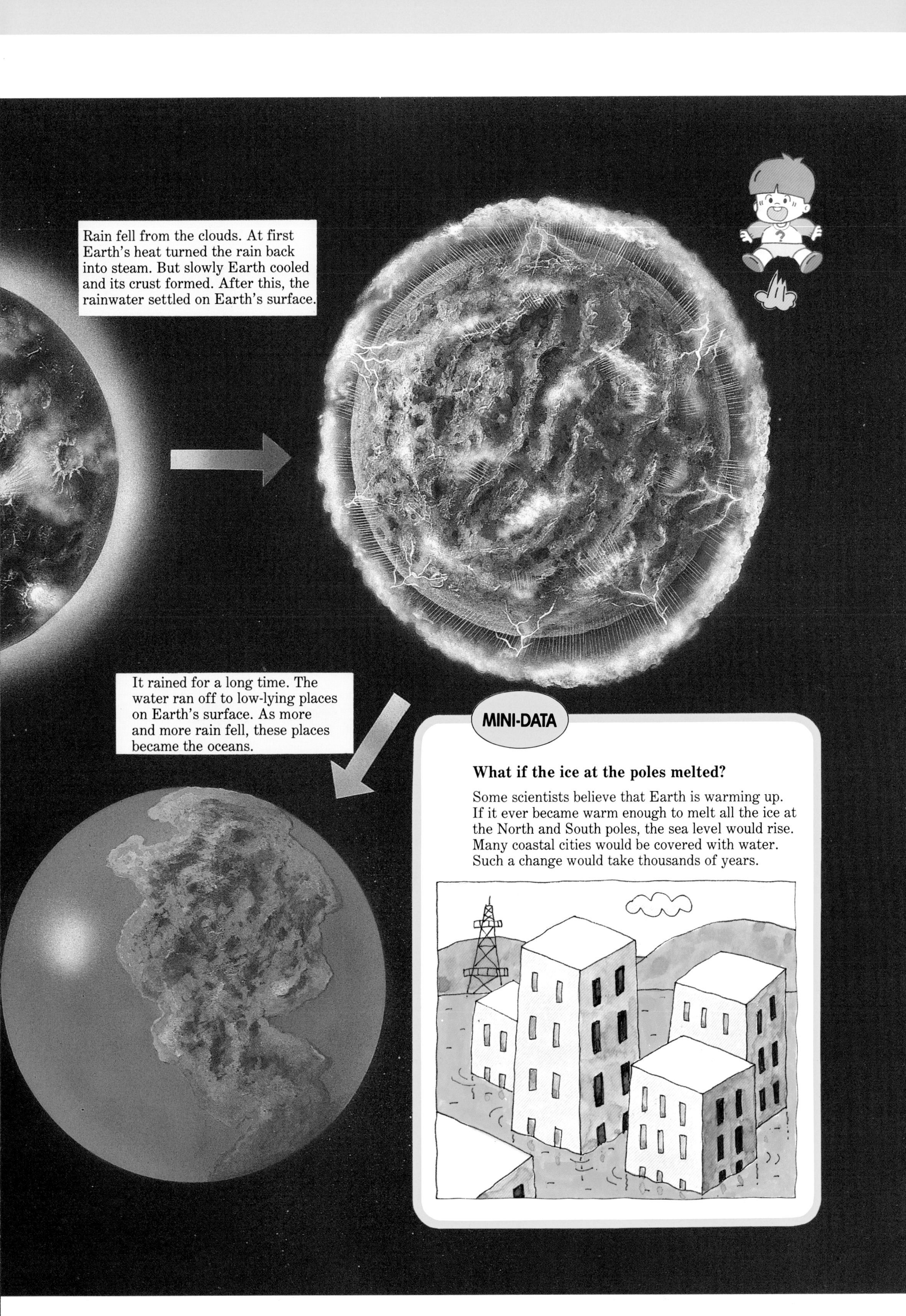

MINI-DATA

What if the ice at the poles melted?

Some scientists believe that Earth is warming up. If it ever became warm enough to melt all the ice at the North and South poles, the sea level would rise. Many coastal cities would be covered with water. Such a change would take thousands of years.

What Is the Ocean Floor Like?

You might think that it is flat, but it is not. Long chains of mountains form mid-ocean ridges that rise as high as 2 miles (3 km) above the seabed. There are trenches too that can be deeper than Mount Everest is high. There are also volcanoes on the ocean floor.

When oceanic plates move apart, they create oceanic ridges. When the plates move into each other, they form trenches. As plates move against each other, they cause terrible earthquakes.

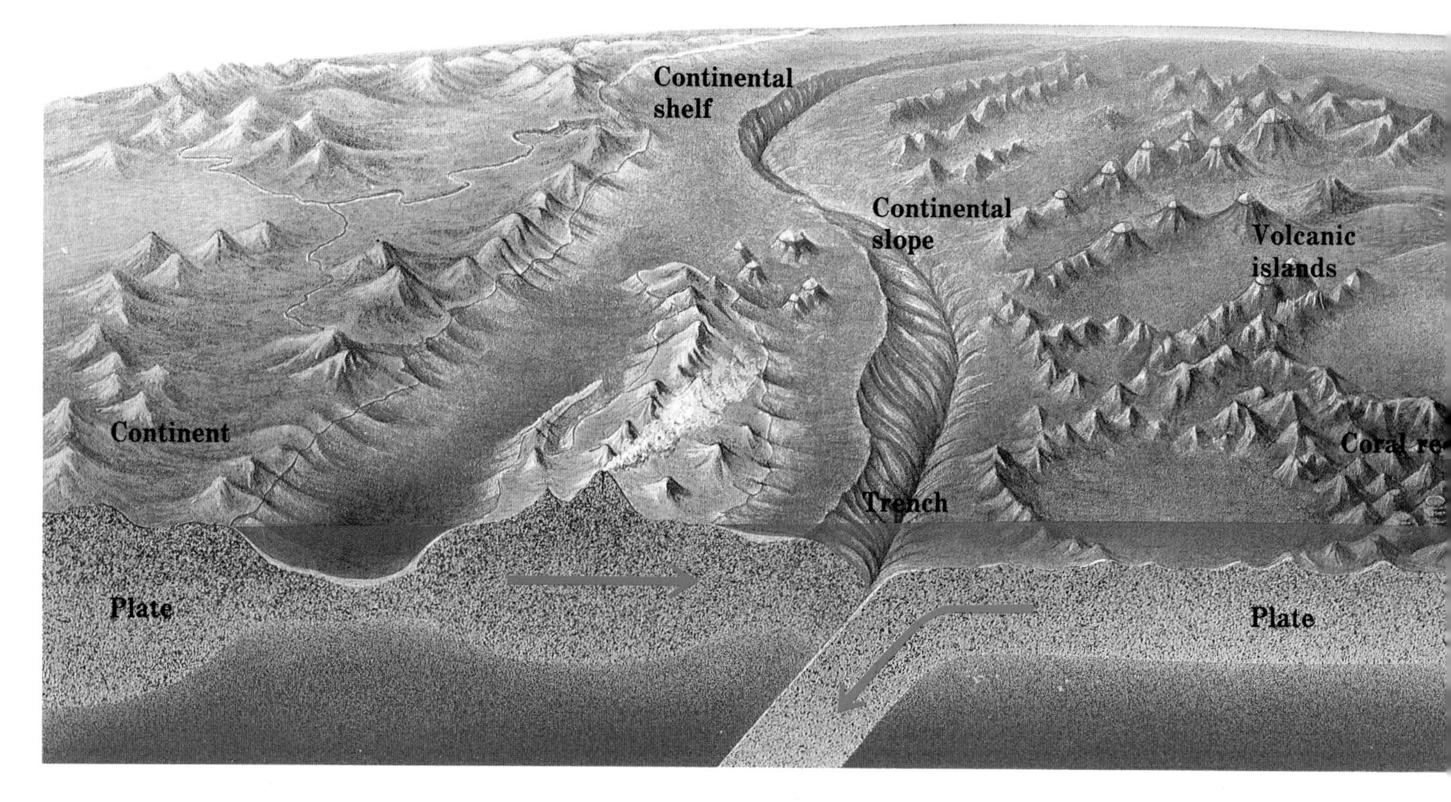

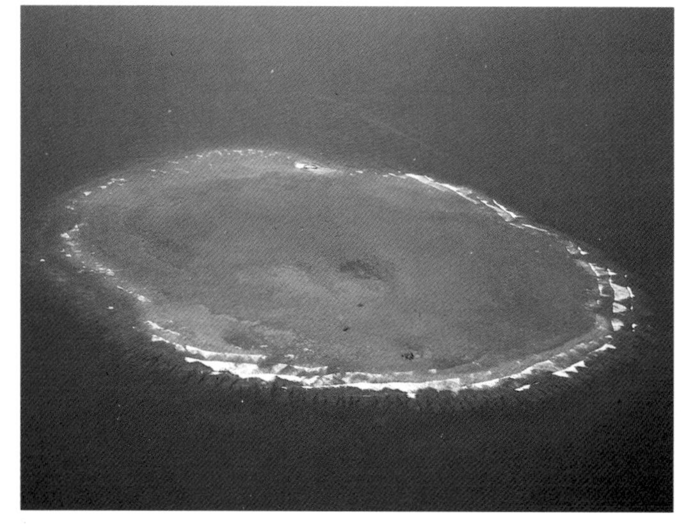

Coral reef

Coral and fish

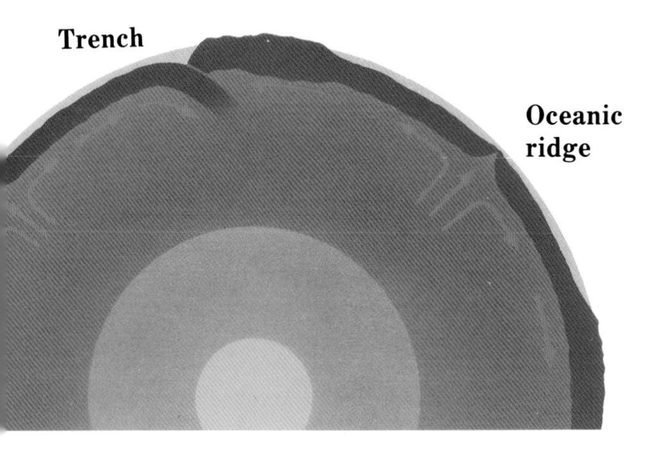

A volcanic eruption at sea

How Deep Can We Go in the Oceans?

In the ocean depths, water pressure is very high. Underwater vessels have to be extremely strong to withstand such pressure. Some of the strongest can dive to depths of 20,000 feet (6,000 m).

• To the Parent

Rising from the ocean bottom is a vast mountain range of mid-ocean ridges, which meanders about 40,000 miles (65,000 km) around the globe. Other features of the ocean floor include deep trenches, plateaus and low-lying basins. Plate tectonics and seafloor spreading are held responsible for this rugged topography. Scientists believe that lava constantly pushes up through rifts in the ridges to spill over on each side. The theory of seafloor spreading suggests that as the lava hardens it forms additional plate material that pushes the existing ocean floor outward until it collides with, and slips beneath, a continent or another oceanic plate. In the oceans, this action creates deep trenches, which can plunge as deep as 7 miles (11 km) below the surface of the sea. Shallow earthquakes occur at the ridges, where plates are moving apart, and at the trenches. However, the strongest earthquakes are at the faults created by plates grinding against each other. Volcanism is also a result of plate movements, taking place both at oceanic ridges and trenches. Mostly this occurs underwater, but in some places the ridge is sufficiently high to break the water's surface. Volcanoes also occur at hot spots within plates.

Did You Know That Oceans Flow?

ANSWER The water in the oceans is constantly moving. It moves in steady flows in particular directions. These streams of ocean water are called currents. All oceans have currents. Strong winds and Earth's spin cause them.

If you put a letter in a bottle and put the bottle in the ocean, the current may take it to another land.

■ Ocean currents

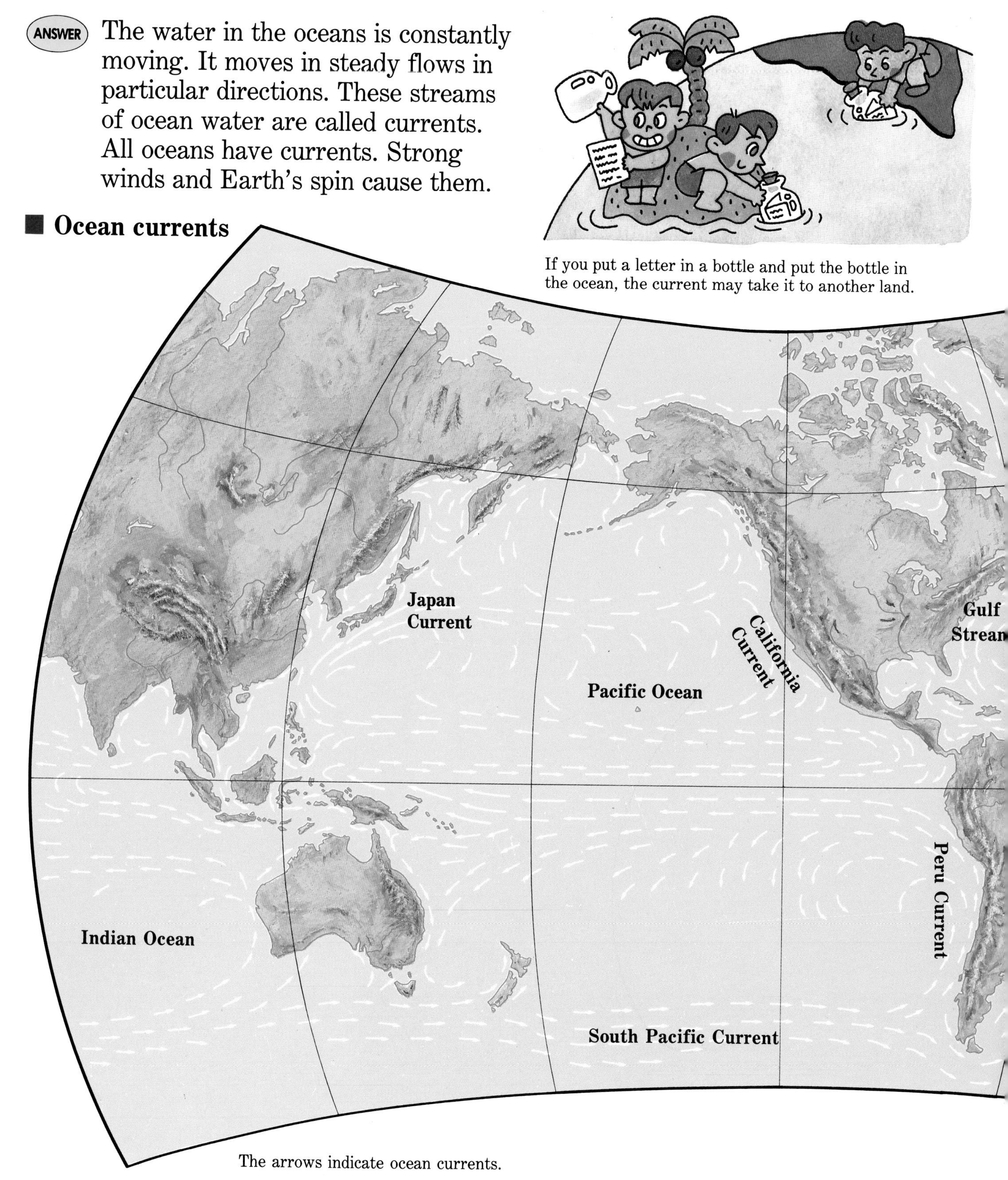

The arrows indicate ocean currents.

• To the Parent

Easterly trade winds cause ocean currents to flow westward at 15° latitude, while westerly winds set up currents flowing eastward at 45° latitude. Meanwhile, the Coriolis effect, a force arising from Earth's rotation, deflects the currents from these straight-line courses to create grand circles, or gyres. These gyres move clockwise in the Northern Hemisphere and anticlockwise in the Southern Hemisphere. Deep ocean currents, though, are propelled by differences in density. The dense, cold water of the Antarctic hugs the seabed as it creeps toward the equator, while slightly warmer water from the Arctic flows above it when the two meet.

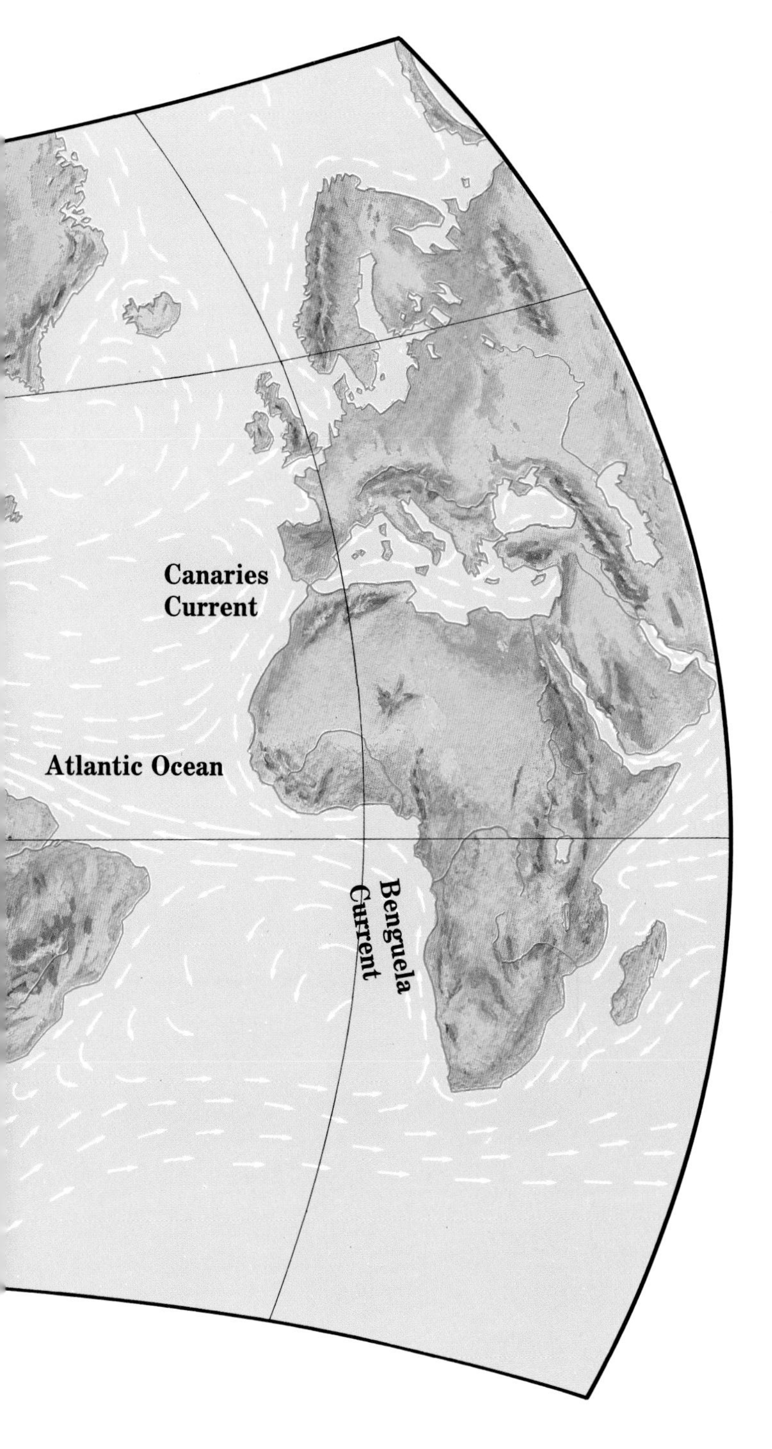

■ Why ocean currents occur

Strong winds set up ocean currents.

Earth's spin bends ocean currents.

■ The direction of currents

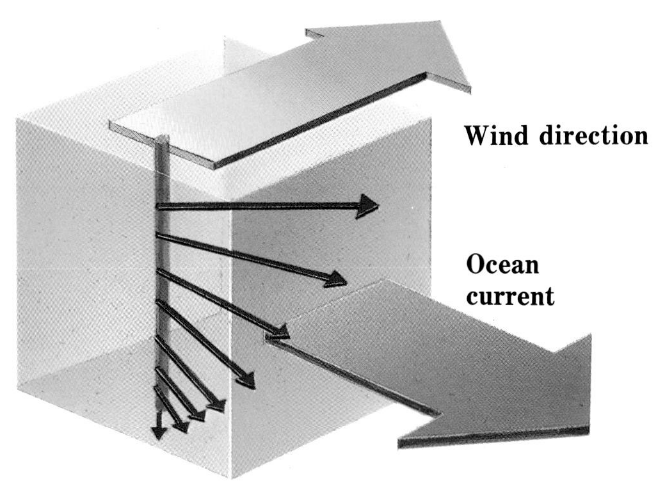

When the wind blows, it pushes water near the ocean surface along with it. But Earth's spin bends these ocean currents. So, water at different depths may flow in different directions.

How Are Rocks Formed?

ANSWER Rocks begin as magma. Magma is hot, liquid rock deep inside Earth. When magma is pushed out of Earth as lava, it cools and becomes solid rock. Other forces, such as wind and water erosion, help change rocks into different types. The photographs below show the three basic types of rocks: igneous, sedimentary and metamorphic.

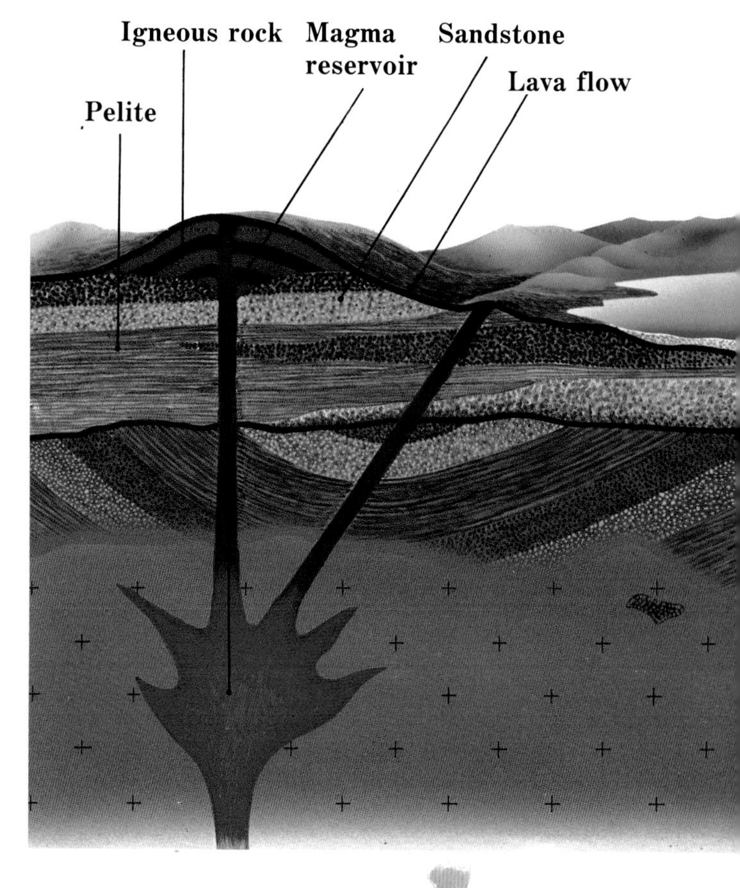

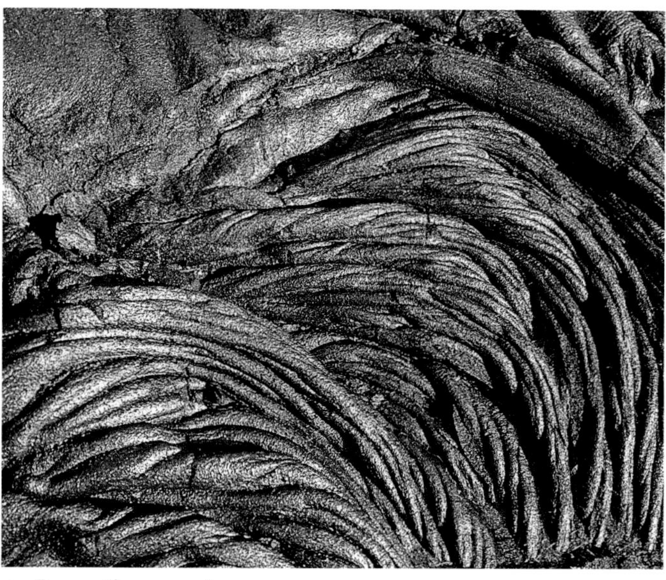

Lava (igneous)

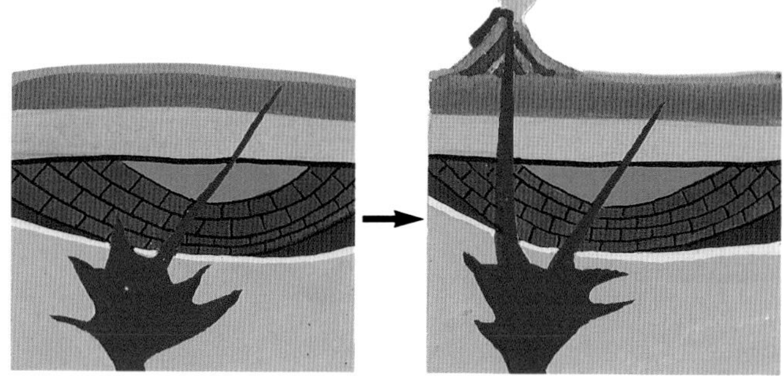

Magma that cools underground or erupts from a volcano becomes igneous rock.

Granite (igneous)

Sandstone and pelite layers (sedimentary)

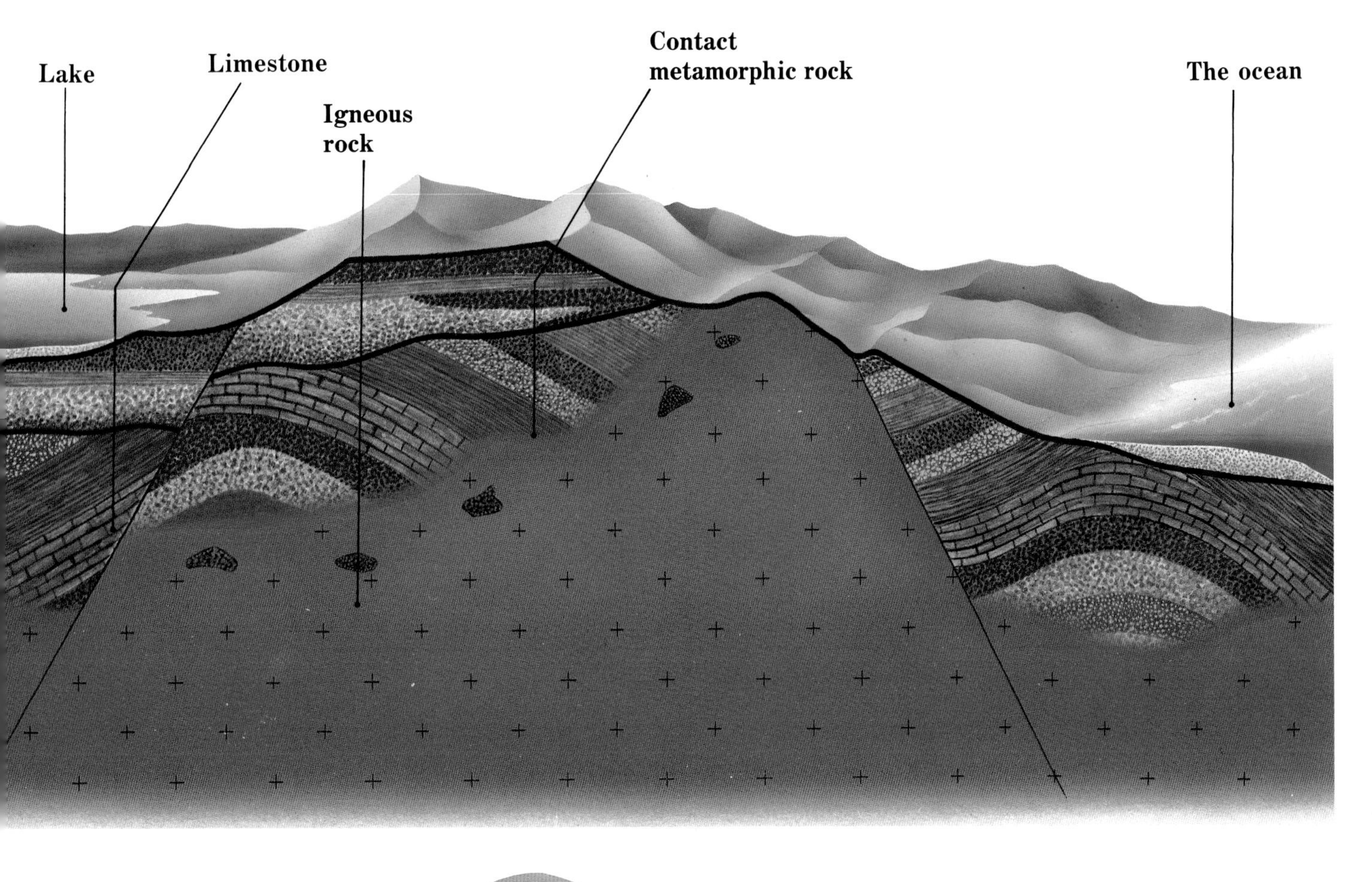

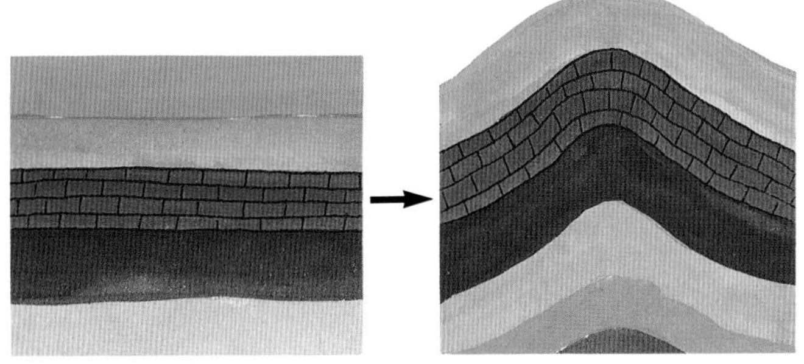

Wind and water erode rocks. The rock particles collect in layers on the seabed. Over time the layers become sedimentary rock.

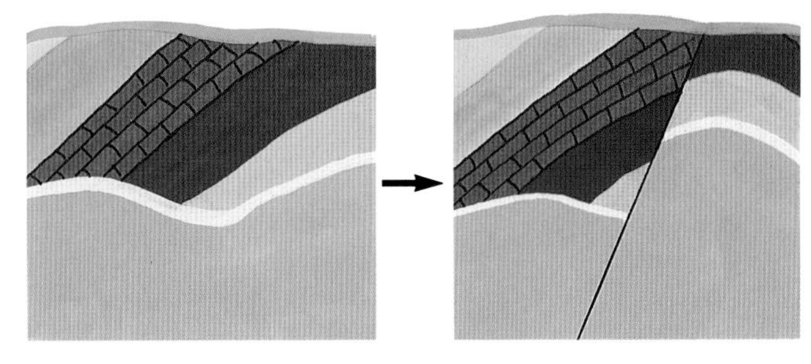

Pressure, caused by movements in Earth's crust, or heat can change sedimentary and igneous rocks into metamorphic rock.

Chalk (sedimentary)

Slate (metamorphic)

• To the Parent

Earth's crust is composed almost entirely of rocks. Igneous rocks that form under Earth's surface and intrude into other rocks are called intrusive; those that form on the surface from volcanic eruptions are called extrusive. Wind and water erode rocks and carry the particles to the oceans, where they collect in layers. The weight of each layer compacts the layers beneath it into sedimentary rocks. Intense pressure, due to geological change, and heat from igneous intrusions or magma can change rocks into metamorphic rocks. These rocks may rise to the surface only to be eroded once more.

What Is Oil Made Of?

How oil was formed

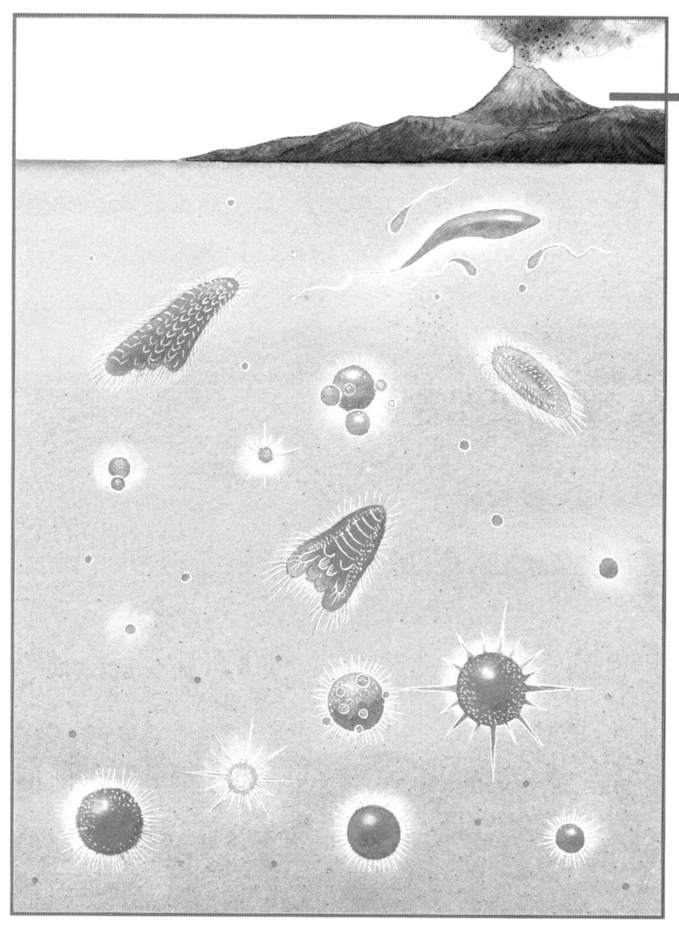

Millions of years ago, water covered much more of Earth's surface than it does today. Living in the water were billions of tiny plants and animals.

When they died, the plants and animals fell to the ocean floor and piled up. Particles of eroded rocks in the form of sand and mud covered them up.

Where oil is found

Areas that contain oil, called oilfields, are scattered about the world. More than half the world's oil is located in the Middle East. Countries that do not have their own supply of oil must buy it from other countries.

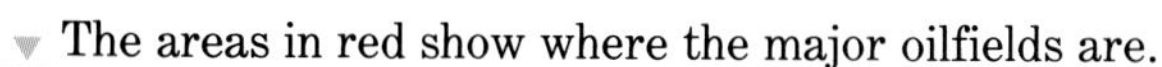

The areas in red show where the major oilfields are.

ANSWER Long ago, when tiny animals and plants in the seas died, they piled up on the seabed. Sand and mud collected on top of them and became rocks. The rocks' weight and the heat from Earth slowly turned the layer of dead animals and plants into oil. This took millions of years.

The layers of sand and mud were very heavy. This weight turned the sand and mud into sedimentary rocks. Heat from Earth and the rocks' weight caused the dead plants and animals to change into oil.

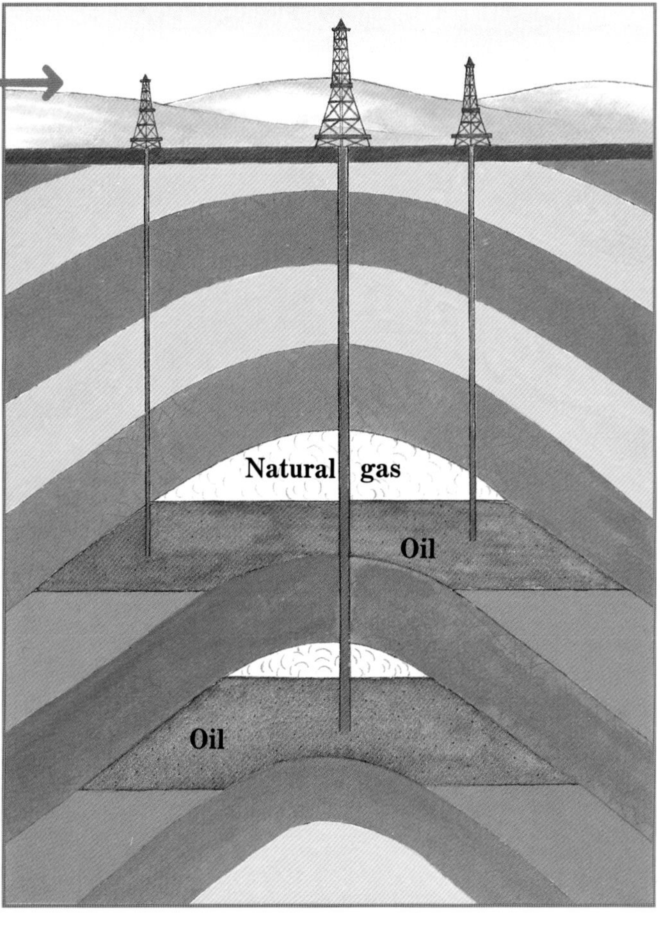

The oil slowly moved up through pores, or small holes, in the layers of rocks. In some cases, it came to rocks with no pores and so was trapped. It is those traps that we drill oil out of today.

■ Getting to the oil

To get to the oil, an oil company must drill down to it. First, a rig is set up to support the drill. Then a well is drilled into the ground until the oil is reached. If the oilfield is in the sea, then offshore rigs are used, like the one shown here.

▲ **An offshore oil platform**

• To the Parent

Geologists believe that the remains of such single-celled planktonic plants and animals as blue-green algae and foraminifera became oil in a process that spanned millions of years. As these organisms died they fell to the seabed and were buried by sediments. Chemical rearrangement and bacterial activity then converted the organisms into kerogen. Thermal action and pressure from layers of sedimentary rocks are believed to have converted the kerogen into crude oil. There is only a finite amount of oil in the world and it is being used up at an ever increasing rate. Other energy sources need to be developed quickly if the world is to avoid an energy shortage.

How Is Coal Formed?

This is how coal is made

Hundreds of millions of years ago, there were many large ferns and other plants growing on Earth.

Plants that died in swamps and on river banks were covered with soil and mud. The dead plants slowly sank into the ground.

Plants that became coal

The coal we mine now comes from large ferns and other plants that grew more than 300 million years ago. In time all of them died. During the many changes in Earth's crust over the years, those plants were buried and turned into coal.

The plants that turned into coal looked like this.

Tree bark fossil

ANSWER Long, long ago plants that died in swamps or along river banks were slowly buried under soil and mud. As the dead plants sank, Earth's heat and the weight of the ground above them turned the dead plants into coal.

As the years passed, the weight of the ground and Earth's heat changed the dead plants into coal.

Coal is usually found in layers, or seams, under the ground. To get it to the surface, we have to dig it out.

MINI-DATA

An easy way to mine coal

There are some places where coal seams are near Earth's surface. Once the soil is removed, it is easy to dig the coal out. This is known as opencast mining.

• To the Parent

A fossil fuel like natural gas and oil, coal is formed by the transformation of organic matter. Plants that lived in vast swamps 300 million years ago are the source of most of the coal that is mined today. As those plants died, they sank into the swamps and were covered with sediments. Gradually they decomposed into peat. As the peat sank, ground heat and pressure removed hydrogen, oxygen and nitrogen from it to leave mostly carbon. This is what we know as coal. Coal is classified by its carbon content—the greater the carbon content, the more heat it gives off when burnt. The lowest grade of coal is lignite, followed by sub-bituminous coal, bituminous coal and anthracite, which is 98 percent carbon.

How Are Limestone Caves Made?

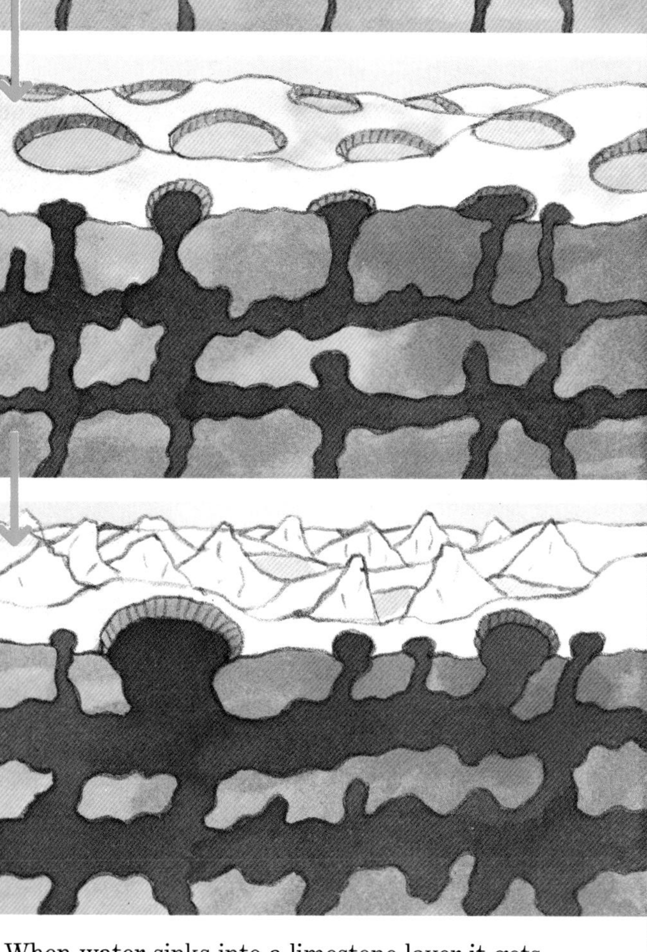

When water sinks into a limestone layer it gets into hollows and cracks. There it starts to wear away the limestone little by little. This makes the hollows and cracks bigger. They eventually become limestone caves.

ANSWER Limestone dissolves very easily. Rainwater that soaks into a layer of limestone will carve out tunnels and holes in the rock. If the holes get big enough they become caves.

• To the Parent

Limestone caves form in two steps. Firstly slightly acidic ground water dissolves areas of limestone bedrock. Since this occurs below the water table the caves are flooded during this process. If the water table falls, the caves drain and the second step begins—ground water seeps into the caves to create beautiful limestone formations.

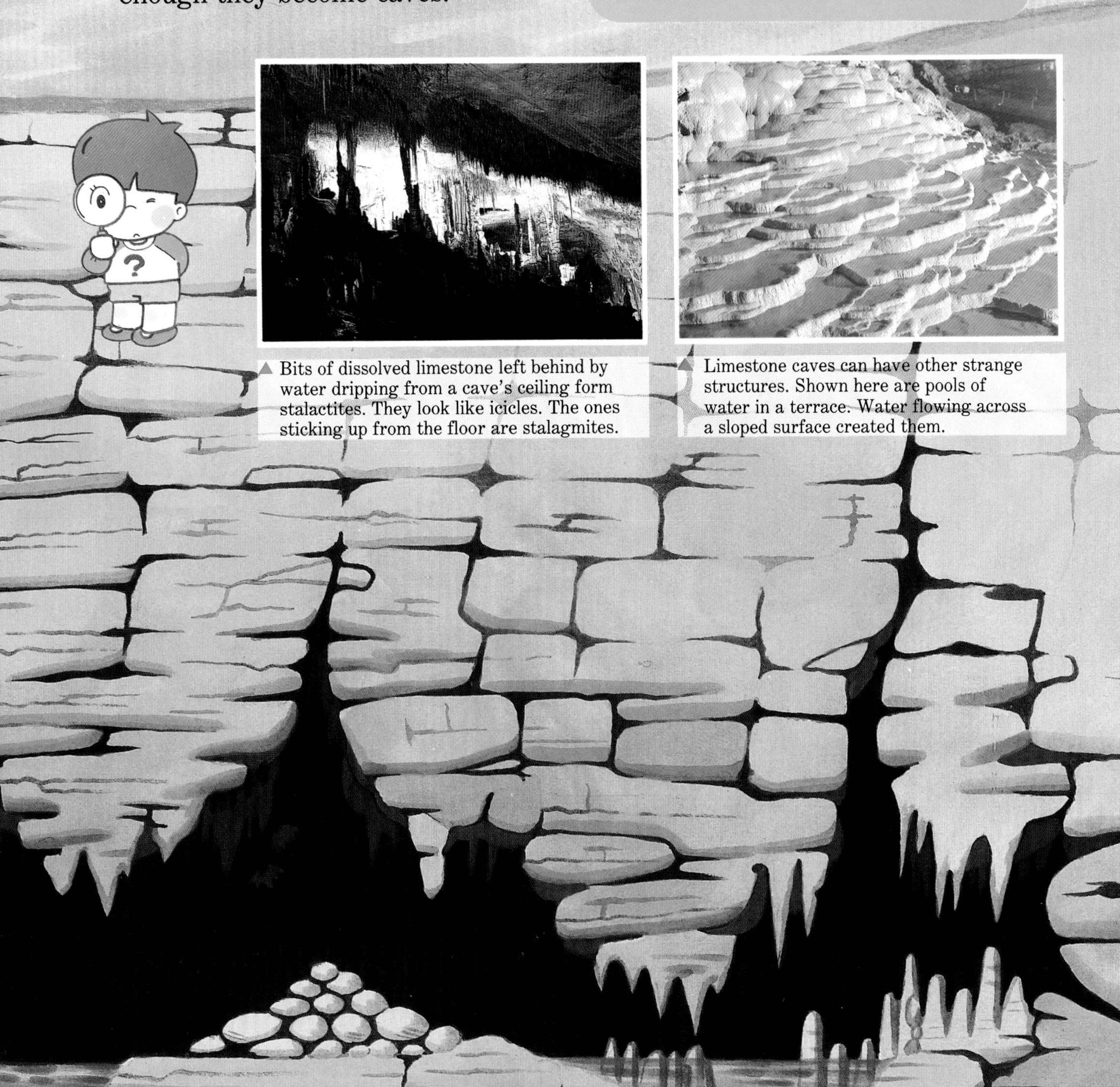

▲ Bits of dissolved limestone left behind by water dripping from a cave's ceiling form stalactites. They look like icicles. The ones sticking up from the floor are stalagmites.

▲ Limestone caves can have other strange structures. Shown here are pools of water in a terrace. Water flowing across a sloped surface created them.

How Does a Geyser Shoot Water So High into the Air?

ANSWER A geyser is a hot spring that spouts water and steam high into the air. It forms when water collects in a hollow deep in the ground. Heated by magma below it, the water in the hollow becomes very hot. It rises to Earth's surface and shoots out.

3,2,1 !

Some geysers erupt at regular intervals.

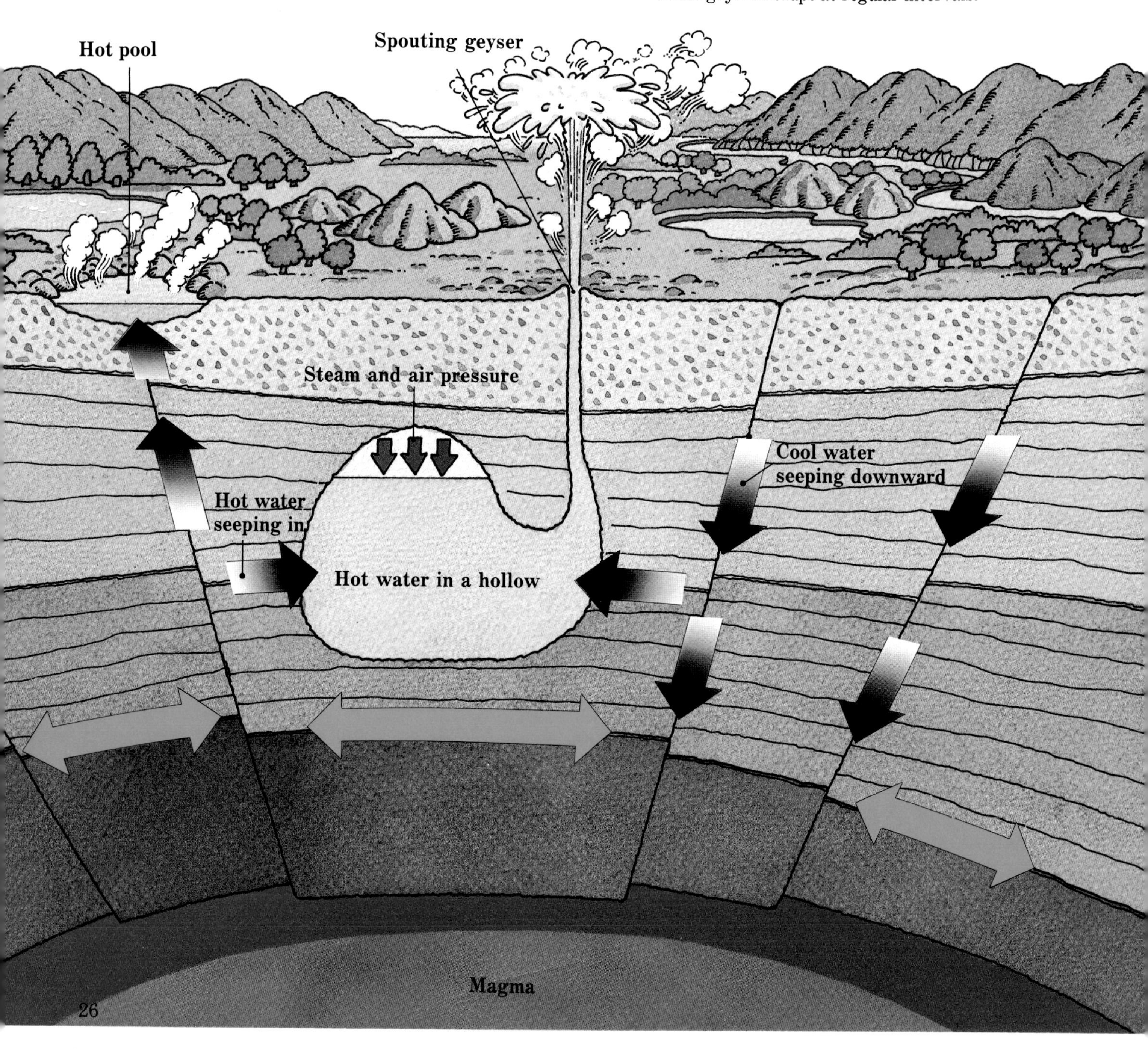

How a Geyser Spews Water

Water seeps into a hollow in the ground. Magma beneath the hollow heats the water and turns some of it to steam. Steam and air pressure build up in the hollow. Hot water rises up the neck of the geyser. When it reaches the surface it spouts high into the air. This happens over and over again.

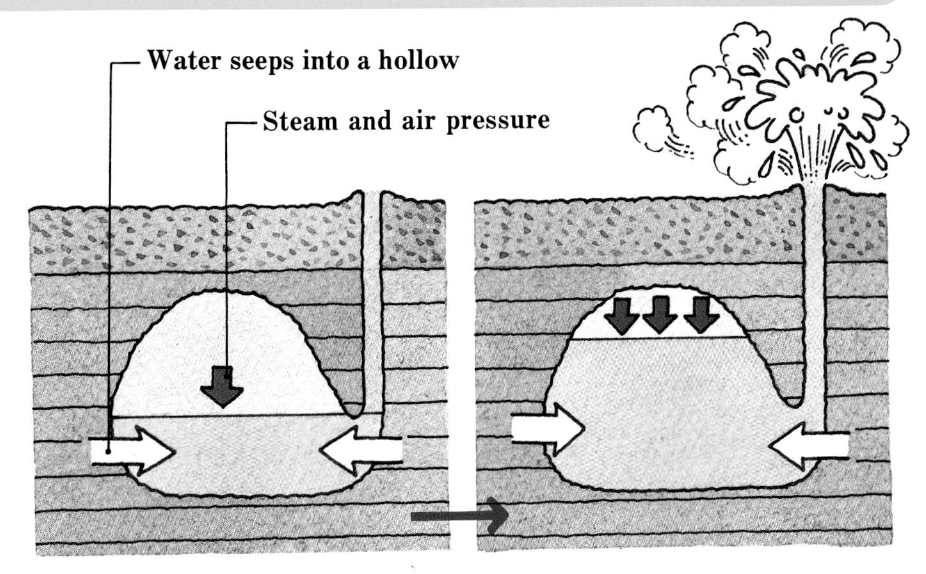

Old Faithful, a Big Tourist Attraction

▲ Yellowstone's Old Faithful geyser erupts about every 65 minutes.

There are 200 geysers and thousands of hot pools in Yellowstone National Park in the northern United States. Old Faithful is the park's most famous geyser. It attracts crowds of tourists.

• To the Parent

Geysers occur in places where Earth's crust is 2 to 3 miles (3 to 5 km) thick. As well as Yellowstone National Park, other such areas include parts of Iceland and New Zealand. Although Old Faithful erupts regularly, most geysers spout intermittently. They may go off several times in an hour or remain dormant for hours, days, weeks or even months. Some spout jets to heights of 1,000 feet (300 m), while others bubble just a few inches above ground.

How High Does the Atmosphere Go?

ANSWER Earth is surrounded by the air we breathe. We call this mixture of gases the atmosphere. The atmosphere is thickest near Earth's surface. It gets thinner with height. There is hardly any air at all above 300 miles (480 km). Scientists divide the atmosphere into layers.

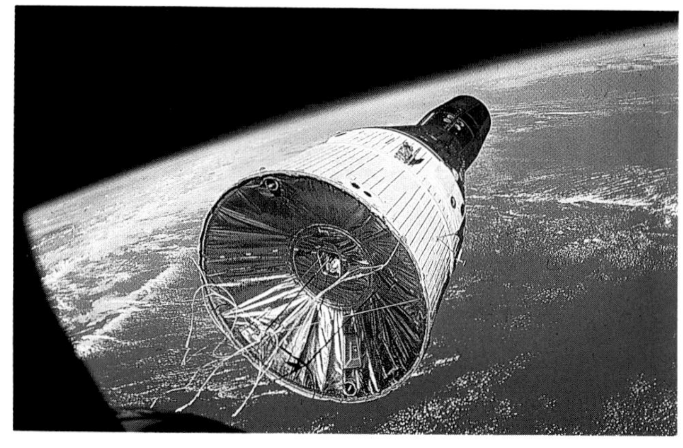

▲ The air seems to be a misty blue on the horizon.

■ The layers of the atmosphere

miles/km

125/200

50/80

30/50

9/15

Ionosphere
The ionosphere starts from about 50 miles (80 km) above Earth. It is divided into several sub-layers. There are many charged particles called ions in the ionosphere.

Shooting star

Mesosphere
The mesosphere is 30 to 50 miles (50 to 80 km) above Earth's surface. It is the coldest region of the atmosphere.

Stratosphere
The stratosphere contains the ozone layer, which shields us from the harmful effects of the sun's rays.

Ozone layer

Troposphere
The troposphere is the atmosphere's lowest layer. It ends about 9 miles (15 km) above Earth's surface. The atmosphere is thickest here.

Gases in the troposphere

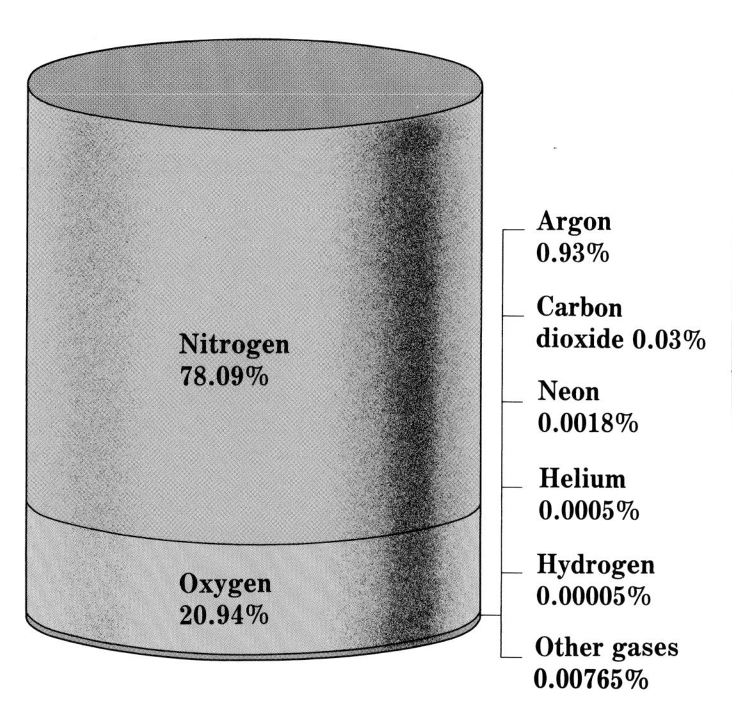

The troposphere is made up mostly of nitrogen and oxygen. It does contain other gases, but they are present in much smaller amounts.

A shooting star glows as it burns

As a meteor from space hits particles of air in the mesosphere it burns up. We call this a shooting star.

What Is Atmospheric Pressure?

Air presses on all things. We call this atmospheric, or air, pressure. At sea level, where air is thickest, air exerts a pressure of almost 15 pounds per square inch, or 103 kilopascals.

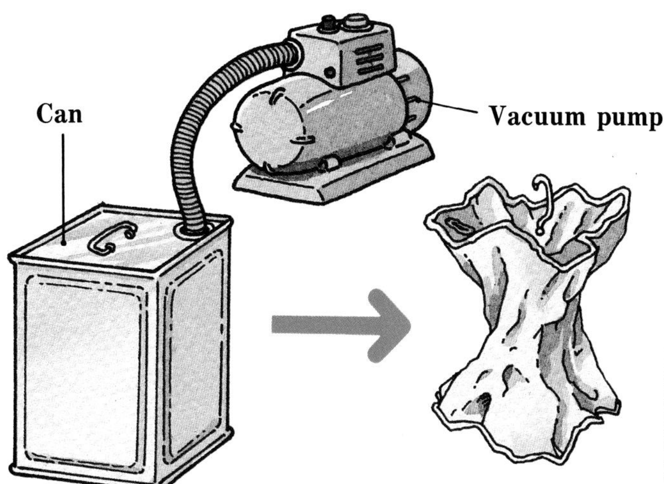

If you pump all the air out of a can, the can crumples up. This is because there is no air inside the can to balance the air pressing against it on the outside.

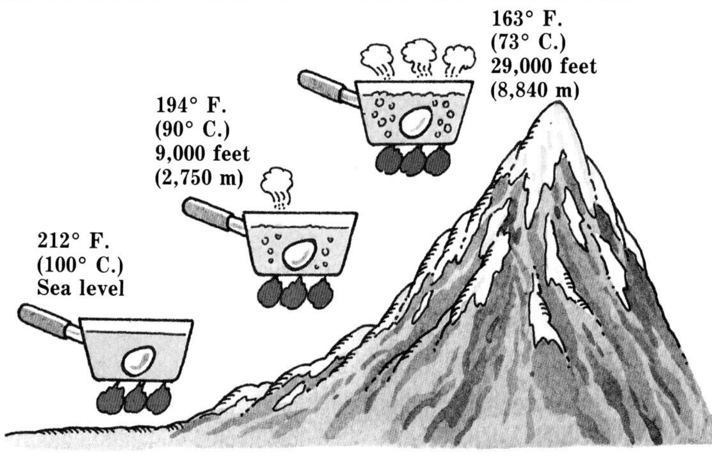

Since air gets thinner with height, the higher you go the lower the air pressure becomes. This affects the boiling point of water. It goes down the higher you go.

• To the Parent

The atmosphere is essential to sustaining life on Earth. People and animals need its oxygen for respiration, while plants require its carbon dioxide for photosynthesis. Also, its ozone layer shields Earth from the sun's harmful ultraviolet rays. Since a liquid boils when its vapour pressure exceeds atmospheric pressure, its boiling point decreases with height due to falling atmospheric pressure.

Why Does a Low-Pressure Area Usually Bring Rain?

ANSWER A low-pressure area is one that has a lower atmospheric pressure than the areas around it. When this happens, air flows into the low-pressure area. This causes air currents to rise. Water vapour in these air currents cools and forms clouds that produce rain.

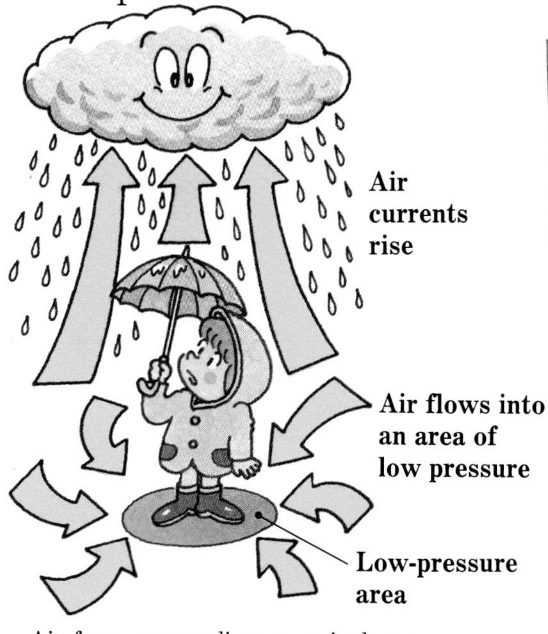

Air from surrounding areas is drawn to the centre of a low-pressure area.

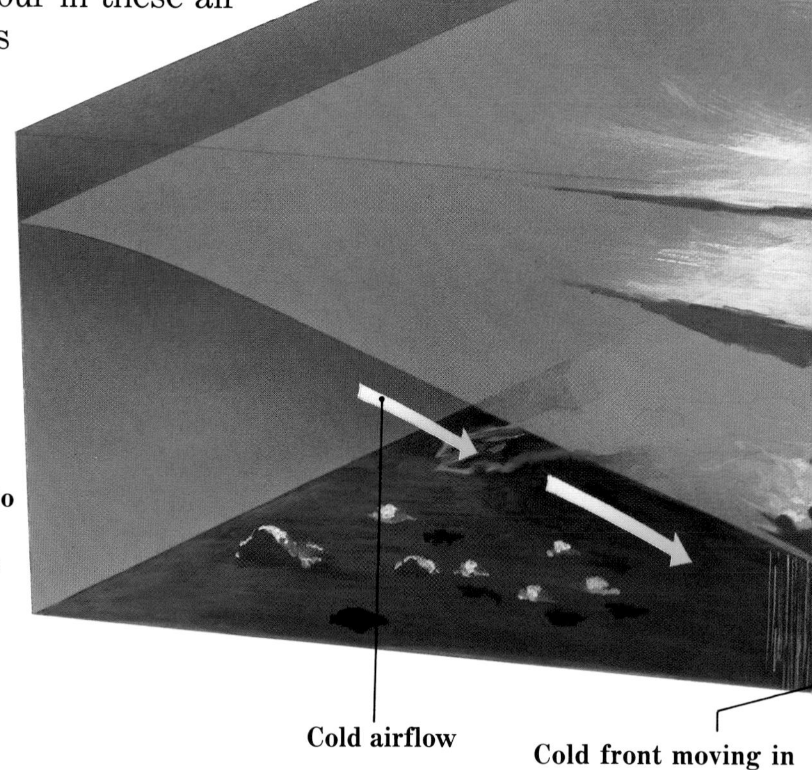

■ Cold and warm fronts

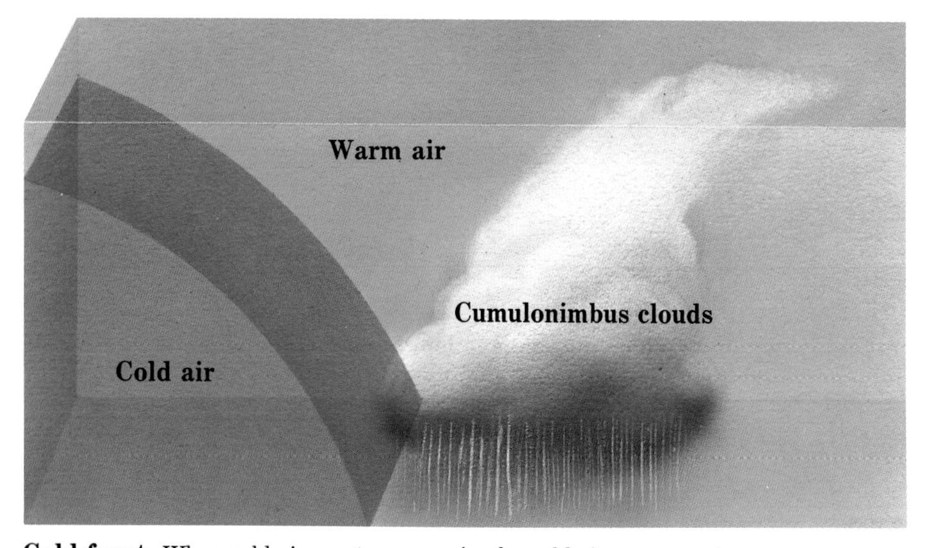

Cold front. When cold air meets warm air, the cold air moves under the warm air. The warm air rises and cumulonimbus clouds form.

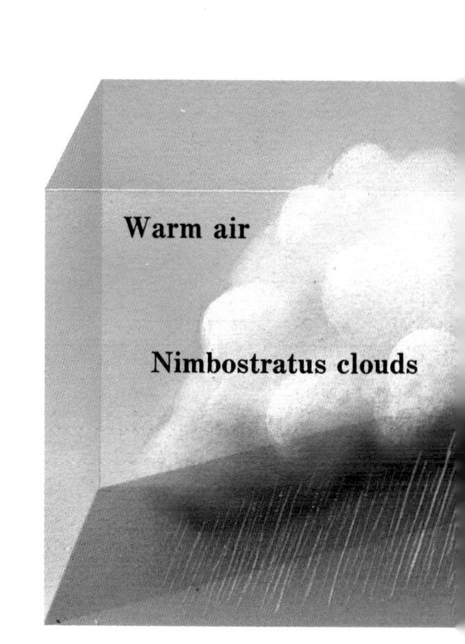

■ A low-pressure system

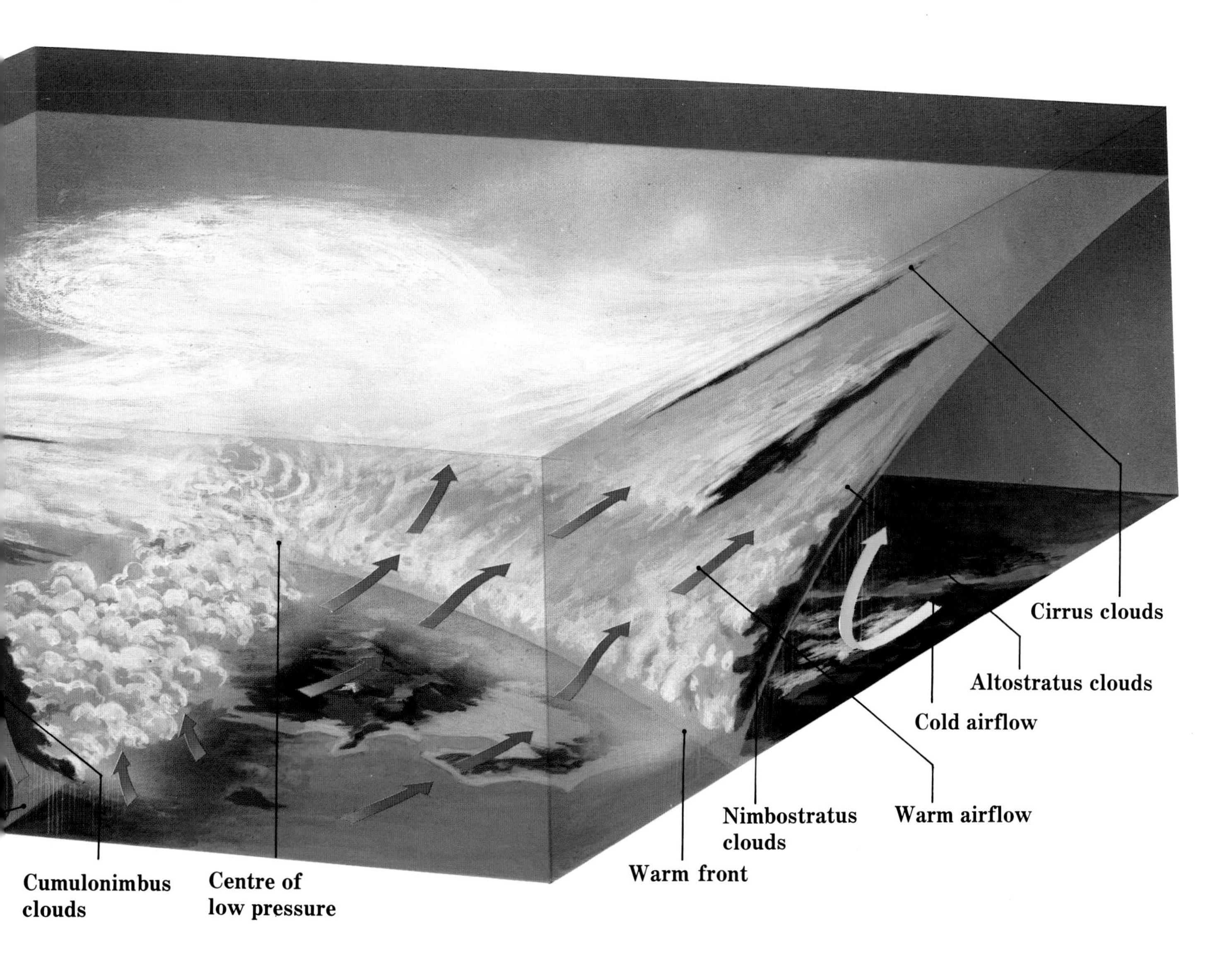

Warm front. When warm air meets cool air, the warm air moves over the cool air. This causes nimbostratus clouds to form near the warm front.

• To the Parent

Most low-pressure systems evolve when westerly winds in the upper atmosphere create a valley of low pressure. Warm air in the east moves into the low-pressure area by climbing above cold air and creating a warm front. Meanwhile, in the west cold air descends in a cold front. As air currents rise along these fronts water vapour collects and condenses to form clouds. To replace the air moving upward, winds blow in from the outside. These winds move in an anticlockwise direction in the Northern Hemisphere and in a clockwise direction in the Southern Hemisphere. This develops into a whirlpool-shaped current, known as a cyclone. In the tropics such a cyclone can become a typhoon, or hurricane.

How Does a Tornado Start?

ANSWER Tornadoes are fierce whirlwinds that occur most often in the United States. When cold air meets warm, moist air, the warm air rushes upward and cumulonimbus clouds form. As the warm air flows upward a downward air current forms. This creates a thunderstorm. If a strong wind blows through the clouds it can twist the rising air currents into a whirlwind. This whirlwind may spin faster and faster until it forms a tornado.

▲ A twister roars across the United States.

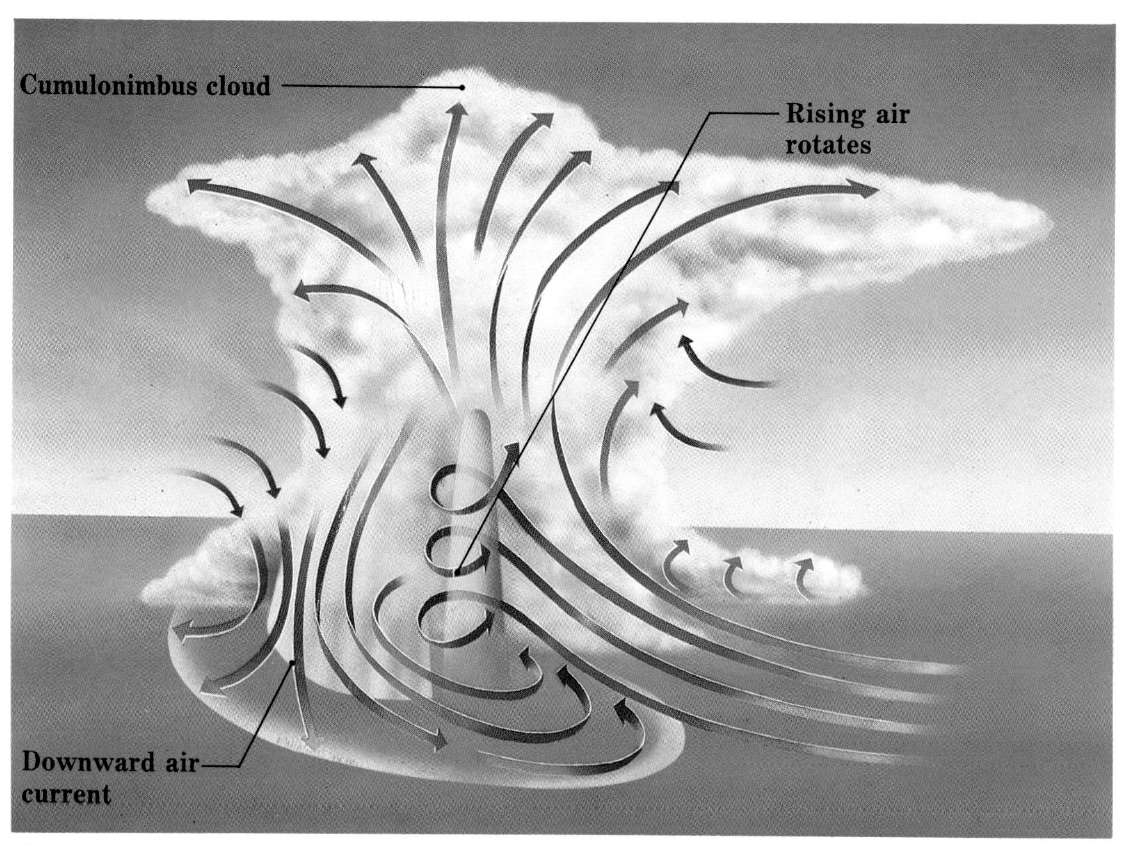

Warm air rushing upward, a downward air current, and wind can give birth to a deadly storm.

• To the Parent

The winds of a tornado are the most powerful on Earth, laying waste to almost everything they come across. As a tornado progresses it sucks air upward. When this happens over a building, the air pressure inside the structure exceeds the air pressure outside. For this reason buildings in the path of a tornado have been known to explode. Most tornadoes occur in the Great Plains of the United States. In 1925, one of the fastest and largest killed 689 people as it travelled 220 miles (354 km) across Missouri, Illinois and Indiana.

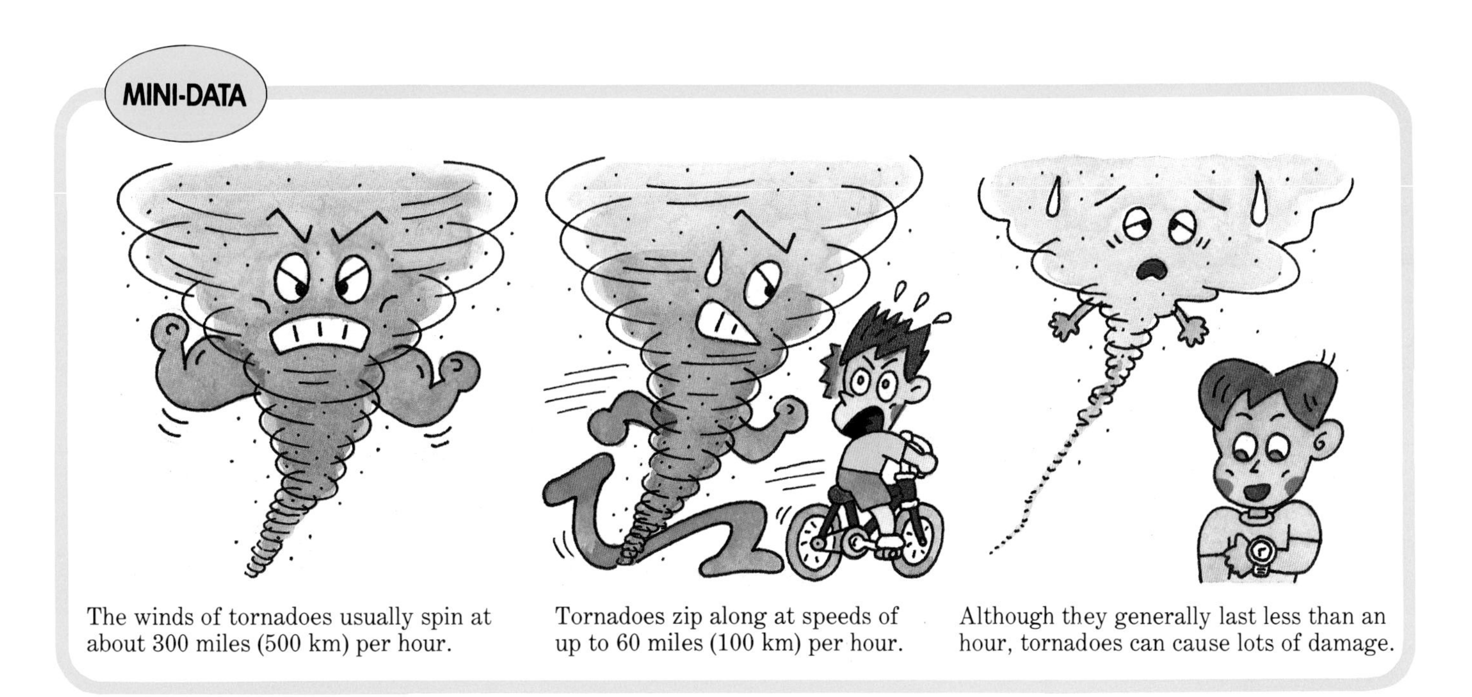

The winds of tornadoes usually spin at about 300 miles (500 km) per hour.

Tornadoes zip along at speeds of up to 60 miles (100 km) per hour.

Although they generally last less than an hour, tornadoes can cause lots of damage.

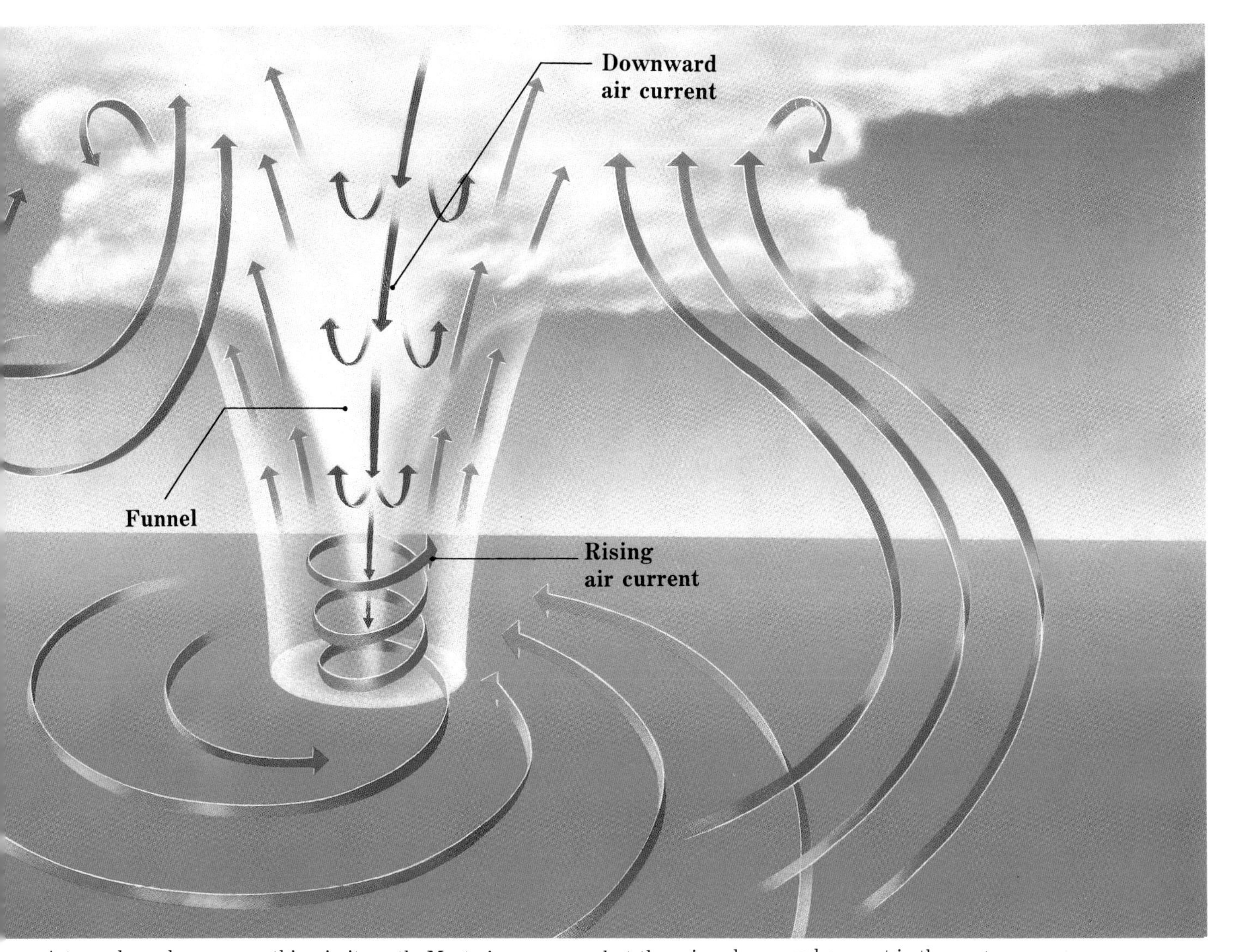

A tornado sucks up everything in its path. Most air moves up, but there is a downward current in the centre.

What Causes a Glacier?

ANSWER Glaciers are huge bodies of flowing ice. They occur in regions where it is very cold, like the North and South poles, and in mountain ranges. Snow does not melt in these places because it is so cold. Instead the snow piles up. As it does so, it crushes the snow beneath it into ice and forms glaciers. The glaciers slowly move downward changing the shape of the land as they go.

I wish I had brought my sledge.

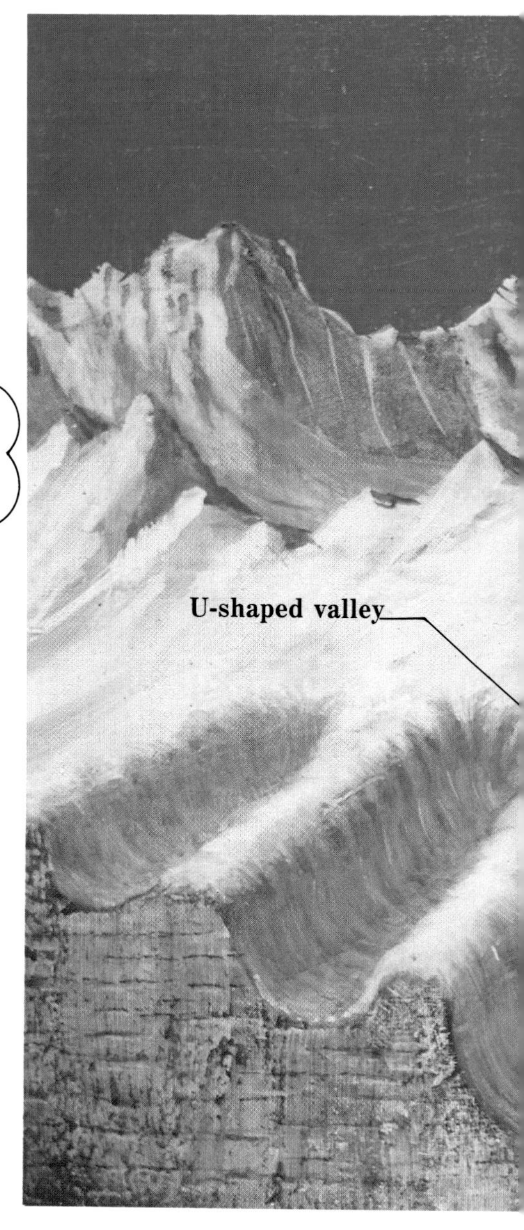

Glaciers moving downward can carve U-shaped valleys.

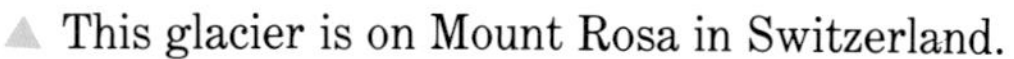

▲ This glacier is on Mount Rosa in Switzerland.

• To the Parent

Glaciers are colossal sculptors of the land. As they advance they gouge out bowl-shaped cirques in mountainsides and carve U-shaped troughs out of existing valleys. These actions create huge quantities of rock debris, which the glaciers transport and deposit as moraines and drumlins. The latter are oval-shaped piles of rock. When a glacier melts faster than it moves it retreats up the valley, leaving behind these features. Another landform associated with glaciers are eskers—narrow ridges of sand and gravel laid down by streams of meltwater that have tunnelled through the glacial ice.

A cirque is a hollow that a small glacier scoops out of a mountain.

The patterns and shapes on a glacier's surface are made by bits of rock carried by the glacier.

Bits of rock carried by glaciers collect to form ridge-like mounds called moraines.

■ Glaciers and the snow line

Above a certain height snow never melts. This is called the snow line. Glaciers form above this line and melt below it.

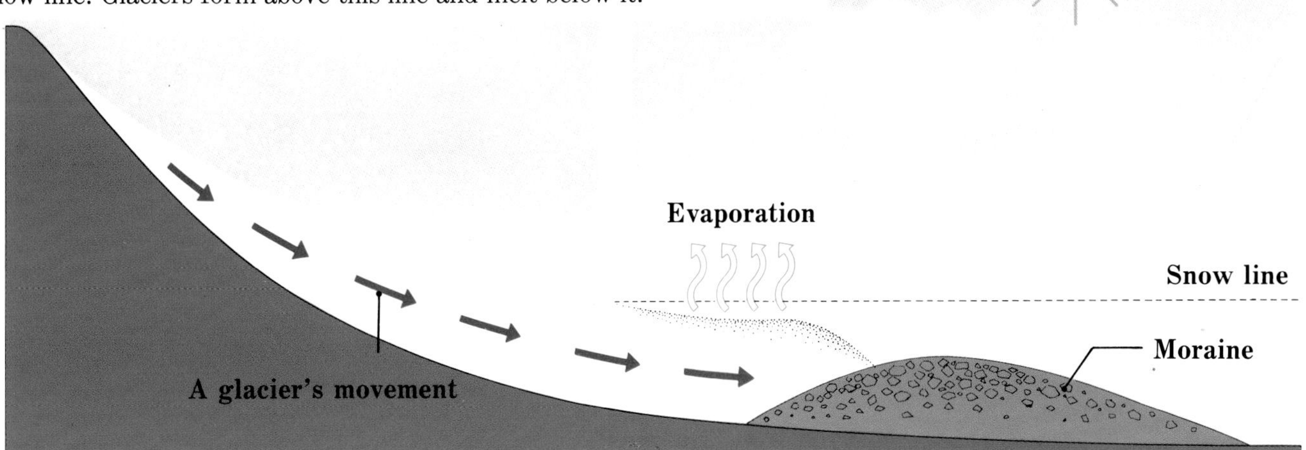

How Are Lakes Formed?

Action by glaciers formed most lakes. Long ago, glaciers gouged out hollows in the land, which filled with water. The bits of rock in glaciers also dammed up streams, which caused lakes to form. Some lakes are made when water collects in the craters of volcanoes. These and other ways that lakes form are shown here.

A dammed lake

If a landslide or lava flow dams a river, a lake may form. Rocks carried by glaciers can also dam rivers to create lakes.

An oxbow lake

When a river cuts a new channel across the neck of one of its loops, it leaves behind this sort of lake.

A dammed lake
An oxbow lake
A lagoon

A lagoon

Coral or a build-up of sand around part of the sea can create a lagoon.

▲ **A lagoon**

• To the Parent

Lakes are inland bodies of water created by the blockage of natural drainage channels or by the accumulation of water in hollows. Examples of how this can happen are given above. Glacial action during the Pleistocene epoch created most lakes. It gouged out deep areas of bedrock, which filled with water when the glaciers melted. Rock sediments carried by glaciers also dammed up streams to create lakes, while melting glaciers left deep pits, called kettle holes, which filled with water.

A crater lake

Water often collects in the craters of dormant or extinct volcanoes.

A lake in low-lying land

Hollows in the land, which glaciers may have made, fill with water to become lakes.

MINI-DATA

America's deepest

The deepest lake in the United States is Crater Lake in Oregon. At 1,932 feet (589 m) deep it is almost twice as deep as the Eiffel Tower is high.

▲ A crater lake

▲ A lake in low-lying land

▲ A dammed lake

Why Do We Sometimes See Mirages?

ANSWER Sometimes when we are outside we see things that are not really there. This is called a mirage. A mirage is a trick nature plays on our eyes. When light passes through layers of hot and cold air it bends. This can fool our eyes into seeing something that does not really exist.

The desert is a mirage maker

People in a desert might think that they can see trees or bodies of water far away.

As they walk toward the trees or water the vision vanishes. A mirage is never really there.

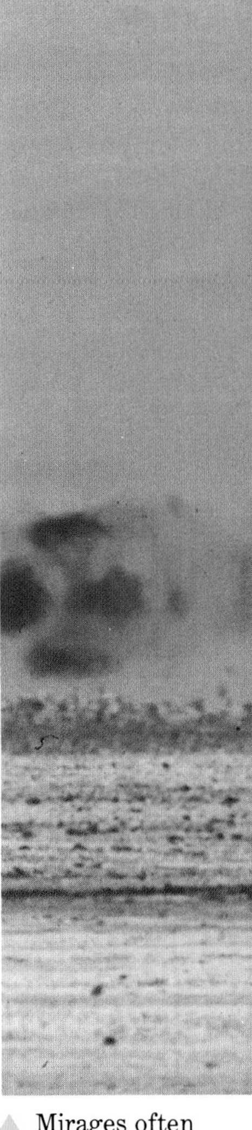

Mirages often

How Layers of Air above the Sea Create a Mirage

When sea water is very cold the air above it becomes cold too. Above this cold layer of air is a warmer layer. Light reflected off something faraway, like an island, will bend as it passes through these cold and warm layers. If this light then enters our eyes, we think we can see the object floating in the sky. It may even seem to be upside down.

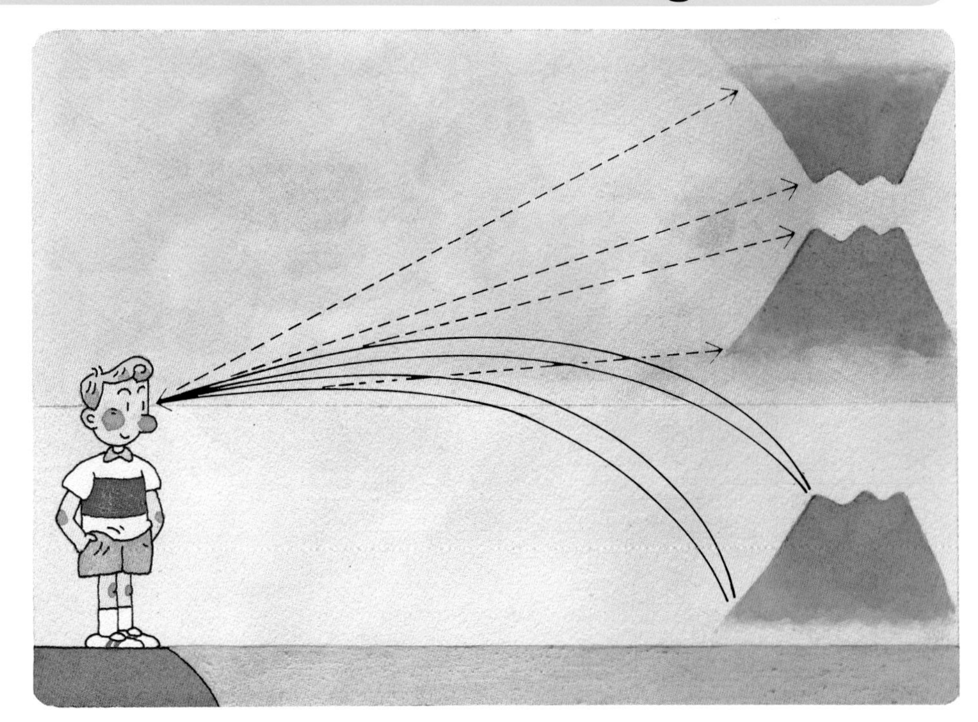

occur on African plains. The air near the ground is very hot and objects appear to float above the ground.

Why We See Mirages on Hot Days

When the air near the ground is very hot we sometimes think we can see a pool of water. The pool is really a reflection of the sky caused by bending light.

▲ That is not really water on the road.

• To the Parent

Adjoining layers of high-density cold air and low-density hot air cause the atmosphere to act like a lens. Rays of light reflecting off distant objects bend as they pass through this lens. Mirages may be upright or inverted, depending on the object's distance and the temperatures of the layers of air.

How and When Did the Universe Start?

ANSWER Astronomers are scientists who study the universe. Many of them believe that the universe began about 15 billion years ago. They think that at first the universe was very, very small and made from completely different materials than it is today. Soon after it began, the universe started to spread out very rapidly. This growth is now called the Big Bang, because it was so fast it was like an explosion.

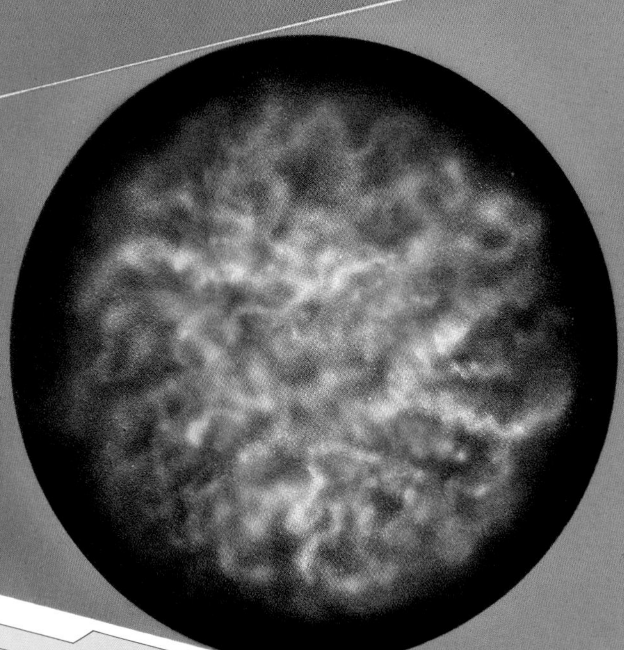

The Big Bang

A million years later

A billion years later

The Big Bang

Before the Big Bang, the universe was the size of a pinhead. Then it expanded so rapidly that it was like an explosion. There was a great flash of light and intense heat of billions and billions of degrees Fahrenheit. There is nothing in the universe today that is as hot as that.

The universe then began to clear up

After the Big Bang, the universe continued to spread out and to cool slowly. At first it seemed a hazy mass. As time passed gases began to form and parts of the universe became clearer.

Huge clouds formed

As the universe kept spreading out, gases came together to form huge clouds known as protogalaxies. The protogalaxies eventually gave birth to stars.

• To the Parent

The Big Bang theory was first put forward by Alexander Friedmann of Russia and Abbé Georges Lemaître of Belgium in the 1920s. George Gamow and his colleagues developed the theory in the 1940s in the United States. No-one has explained, though, how the very dense entity that started it all came into existence or why the Big Bang took place. Many astronomers believe that the universe is still expanding and that it will never stop.

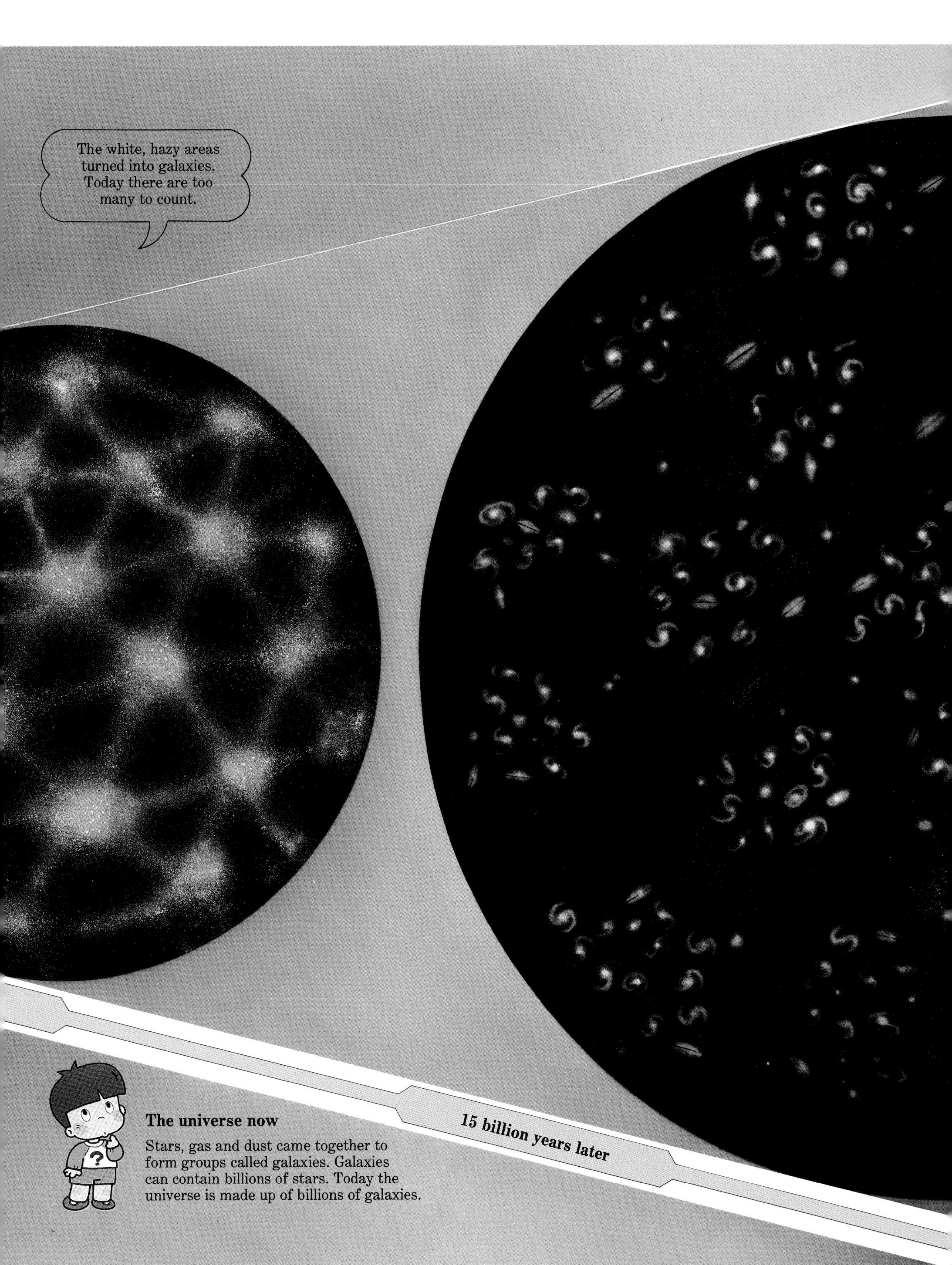

The universe now

Stars, gas and dust came together to form groups called galaxies. Galaxies can contain billions of stars. Today the universe is made up of billions of galaxies.

What Makes an Eclipse of the Moon?

ANSWER Sometimes Earth moves between the sun and the moon. This stops sunlight from getting to the moon and the moon falls into Earth's shadow. We call this an eclipse.

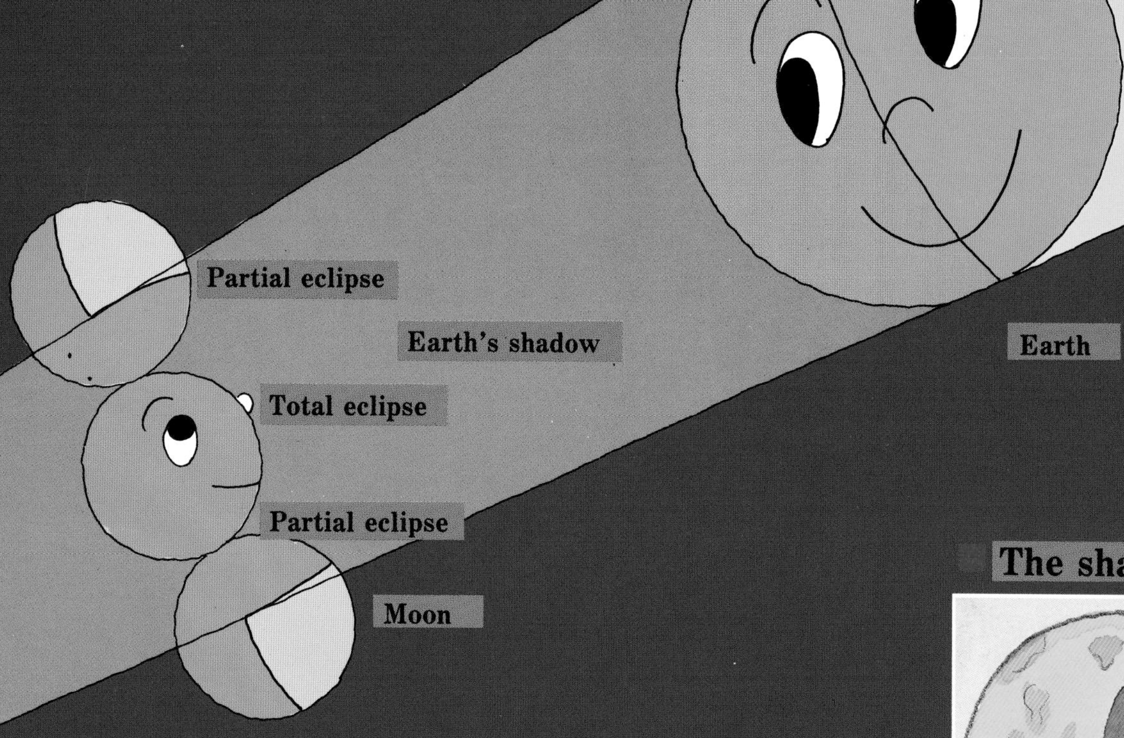

The shadow shows

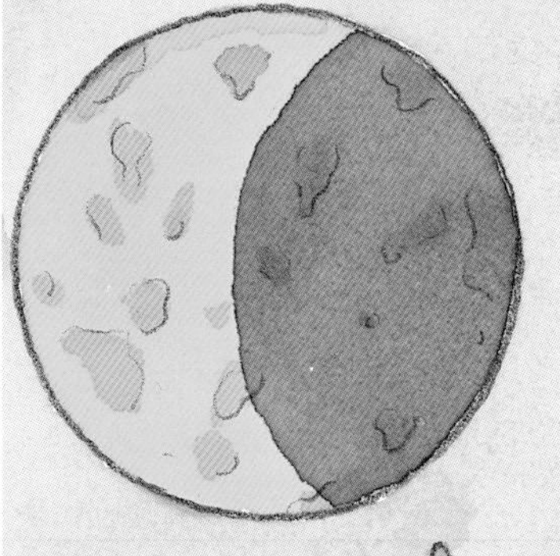

When there is an eclipse of the moon, you can see Earth's shadow on the moon's surface. From the shape of the shadow you can see that Earth is round.

A total eclipse hides the moon.

A partial eclipse hides only part.

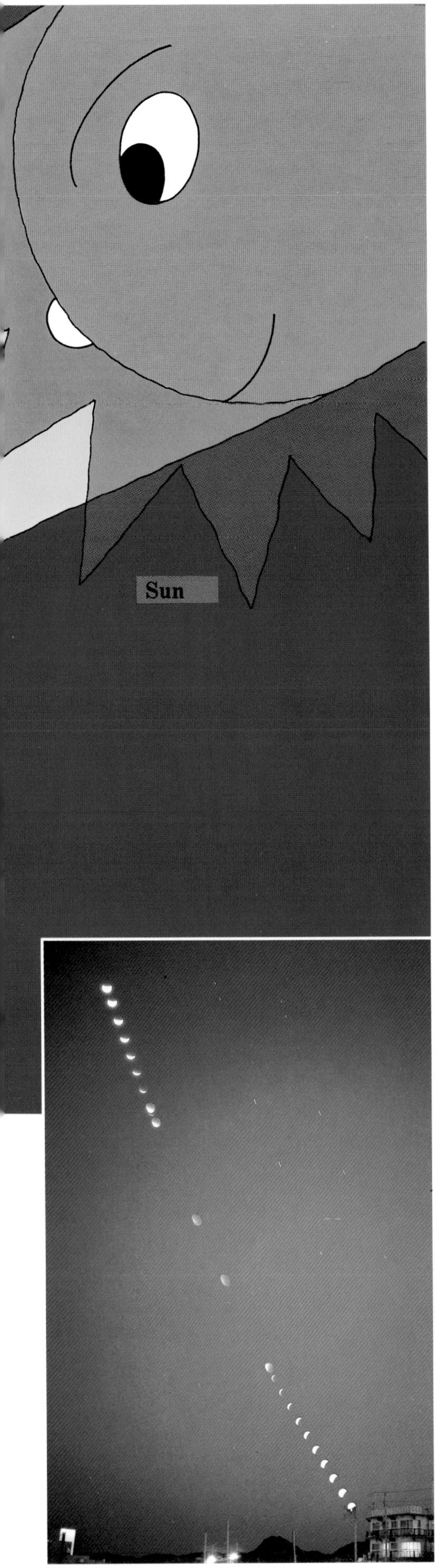

Your own eclipse

A house that blocks sunlight casts a shadow on the street. A child walking into the shadow is in darkness just like the moon during an eclipse.

Why eclipses occur

The moon circles Earth and Earth circles the sun. Now and again all three form a line with Earth in the middle. When this happens Earth's shadow falls on the moon.

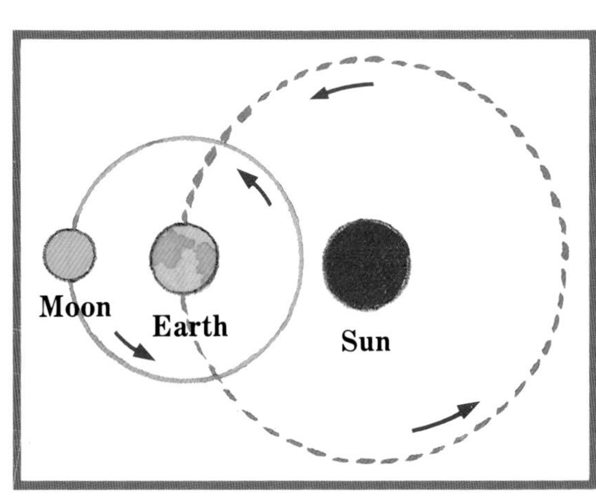

◀ **Progress of an eclipse of the moon**

During the total eclipse, in the middle of this picture, the moon looks red not black. Sunlight contains all the colours of the rainbow. Earth's atmosphere bends and scatters the colours. Red travels farther than the other colours, so only it gets into the shadow.

• To the Parent

As well as lunar eclipses, solar eclipses also occur—when the moon passes between the sun and Earth. One might expect there to be lunar and solar eclipses every month since that is the length of time it takes the moon to complete one orbit of Earth. However, the moon's orbital plane tilts about 5° away from Earth's and the lunar orbit varies. Usually, there are just two to four solar eclipses and up to three lunar eclipses annually.

How Far Away Are the Stars?

ANSWER That depends on the star. The sun is the nearest star to Earth. Its light reaches us in less than nine minutes. Other stars are so far away that their light takes years to reach us.

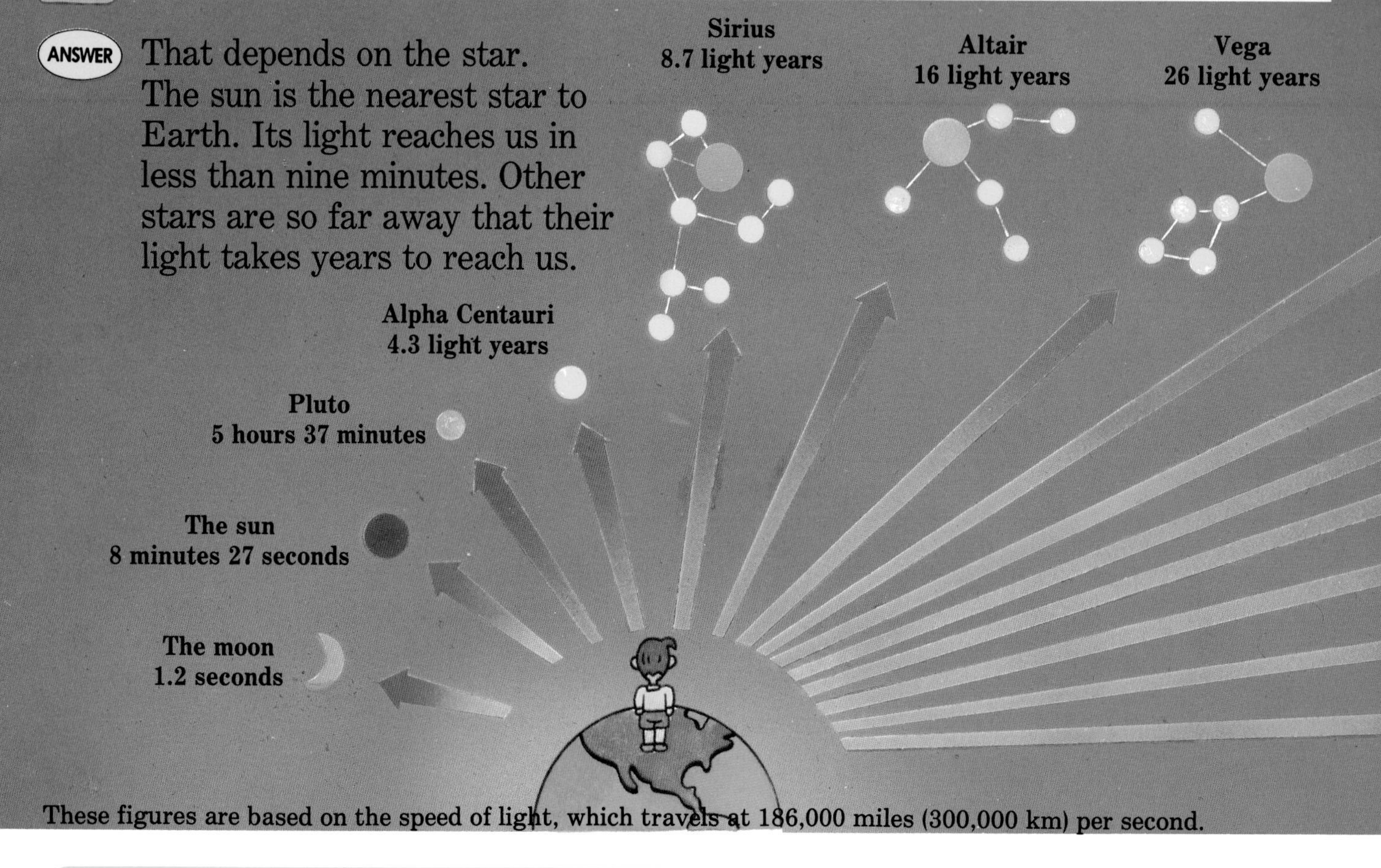

These figures are based on the speed of light, which travels at 186,000 miles (300,000 km) per second.

How to Measure a Star's Distance

When we know one distance we can often use it to figure out another. Suppose two people stand apart and face a tree. We know how far apart the people are. We can also measure the angle they form with the tree, labelled C in the diagram. Knowing these things, we can work out what distance the people are from the tree. We measure distances to stars the same way. We know the distance from Earth to the sun. We measure the angle of a star to Earth on opposite sides of Earth's orbit around the sun. We then use mathematics to figure out how far away the star is from Earth.

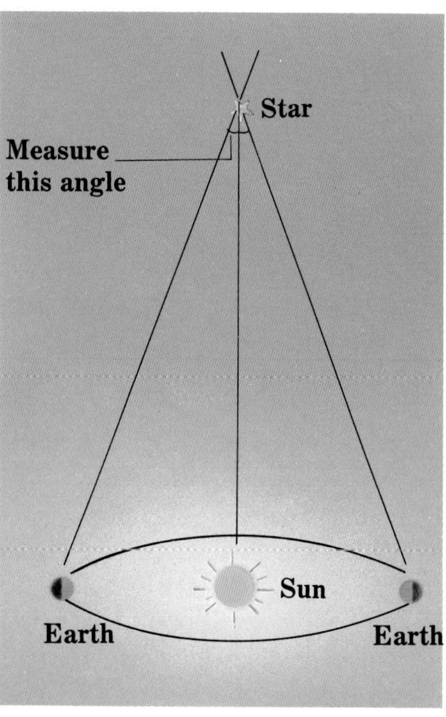

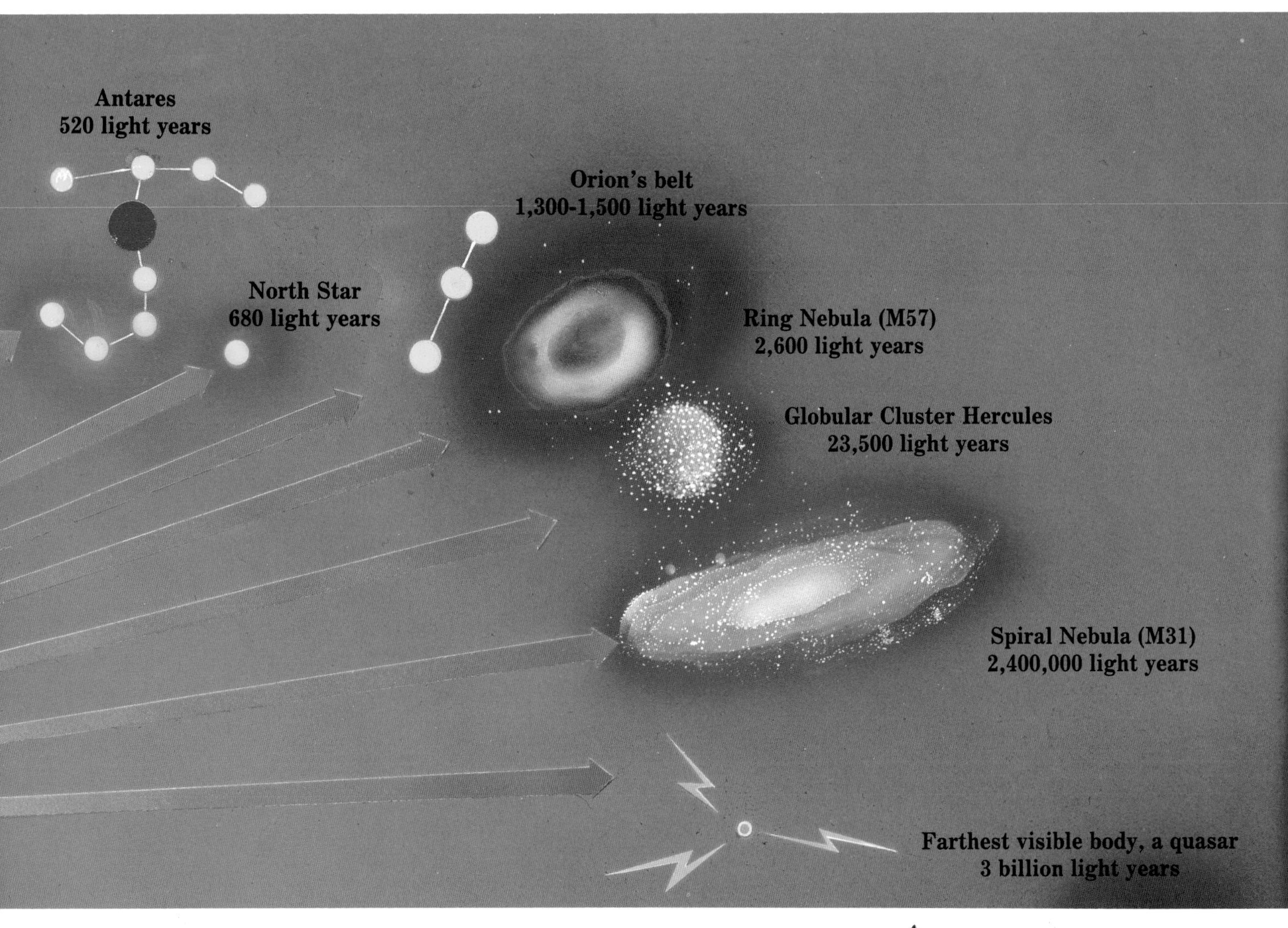

■ Another way to measure distance

Astronomers sometimes measure a star's distance from Earth by studying its brightness. The farther away a star is, the less bright it is.

• To the Parent

The angle subtended at a star by Earth's orbit is called a parallax. Knowing this angle allows astronomers to calculate a star's distance from Earth by using triangulation. However, this method is only useful for the closest stars, which have a large parallax. For faraway stars, astronomers compare a star's luminosity (its actual brightness) with its apparent brightness to calculate its distance.

Why Do People Float inside a Spacecraft?

ANSWER Earth pulls everything to it. This force is called gravity and it gets less the farther away you are from Earth. But even a long way from Earth there is still enough gravity to keep a spacecraft in orbit. Because of gravity's pull the spacecraft and everything in it "fall" around the planet. When things fall they have no weight. This is why people float inside a spacecraft.

As long as the apple and the scale are falling, the apple's weight is zero.

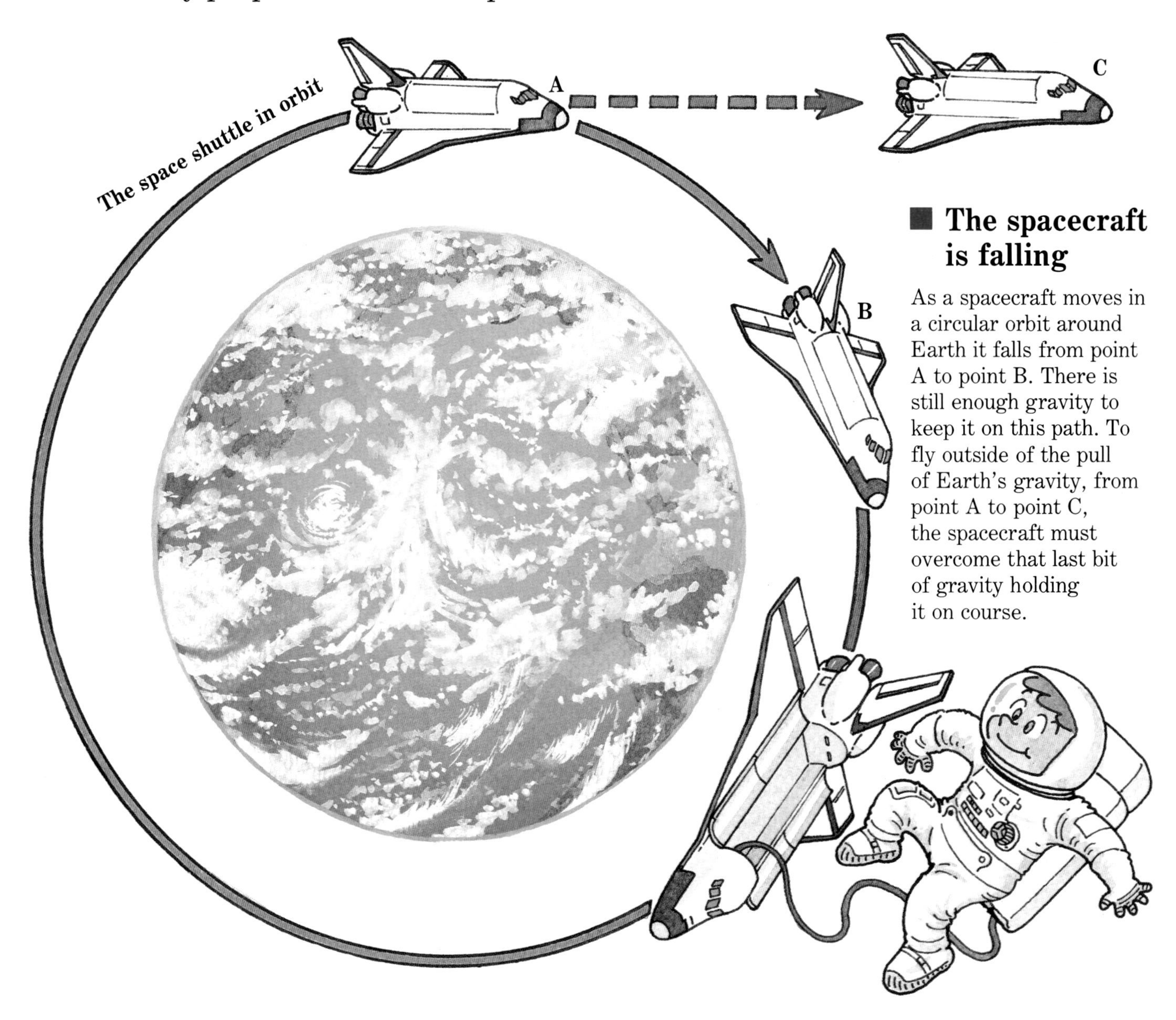

The spacecraft is falling

As a spacecraft moves in a circular orbit around Earth it falls from point A to point B. There is still enough gravity to keep it on this path. To fly outside of the pull of Earth's gravity, from point A to point C, the spacecraft must overcome that last bit of gravity holding it on course.

Strange Things Happen When You're Weightless

Gravity is stronger near Earth's surface than in space. That is why things fall to the ground on Earth. In space, though, objects and people float.

Anything that is not tied down will float. If you let go of things they will start floating.

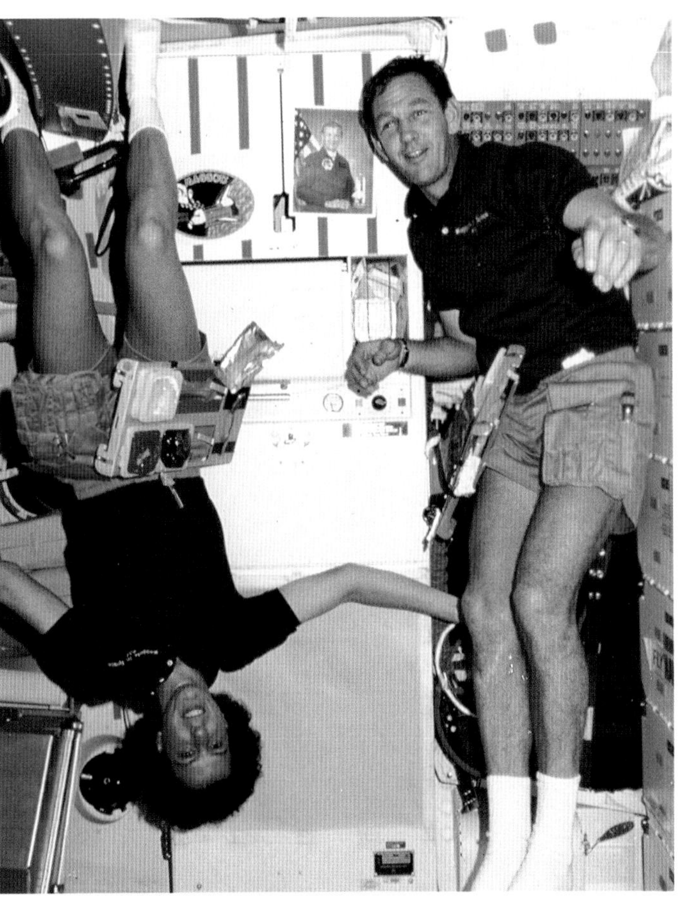

These astronauts are enjoying a weightless meal.

A weightless spider spins a web

An American high school student named Judith Miles suggested an experiment to be done in the space shuttle. She wanted to know whether a spider could spin a web in the weightless conditions of space. The first time the spider tried, it couldn't spin a web. The second time it tried, it was successful.

Spinning a weightless web

In space, water separates into drops that float around in front of you.

• To the Parent

A spacecraft in orbit around Earth is in a free fall along a path that corresponds to Earth's curvature. This neutralizes the effect of gravity in the spacecraft and a state of weightlessness results. How astronauts sleep, eat and exercise are all affected. Foods that crumble must be ground into a paste and sucked through a straw. When they sleep, astronauts have to strap themselves into sleeping bags attached to bunks. And to prevent their muscles becoming flabby, people in space must exercise for about 30 minutes a day.

How Many Colours Does Sunlight Have?

ANSWER The light that comes from the sun is a mixture of red, orange, yellow, green, blue, indigo and violet light. They are the same colours you see in a rainbow. With a prism you can see those seven colours separately. When sunlight goes through a prism it bends so that each colour comes out at a different angle. Violet light bends the most and red light bends the least.

▲The seven colours separate when they go through a prism.

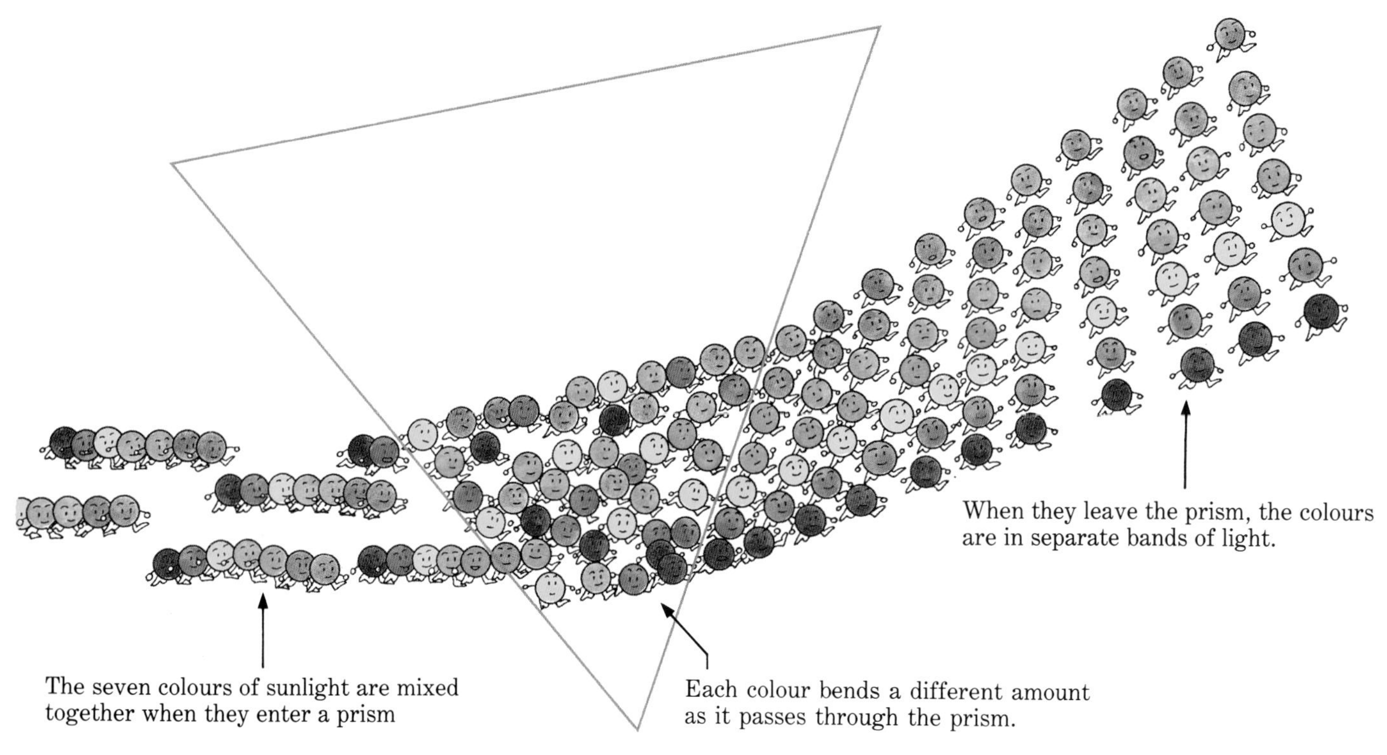

CHECK IT OUT

Make your own rainbow

Sometimes you can see a rainbow in the sky after it stops raining. The rainbow is formed as sunlight passes through raindrops. Like thousands of tiny prisms the raindrops make the light separate into seven colours. Did you know that you can create the rainbow's colours yourself? Here are three ways.

Tilt a mirror in a bowl of water so that it reflects sunlight onto a wall. You see seven separate colours.

Stand with your back to the sun and sprinkle water from a watering can. You can see a rainbow in the drops of water.

If sunlight passes through a small hole onto a round flask of water, you'll see the seven colours reflected.

Why Don't We Usually See Sunlight as Seven Colours?

When the colours of sunlight are all mixed up they look white. That is how we normally see sunlight. You can show how colours mix to form white by making a spinning top. Cut out a circle from card and paint it the colours of the rainbow: red, orange, yellow, green, blue, indigo and violet. Stick a pencil through the card's middle and spin it. It looks white.

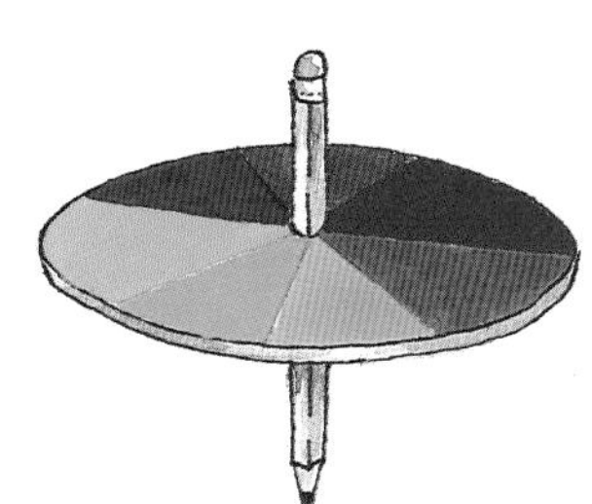

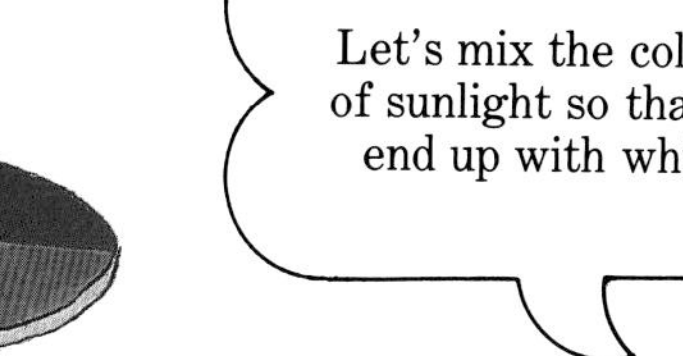

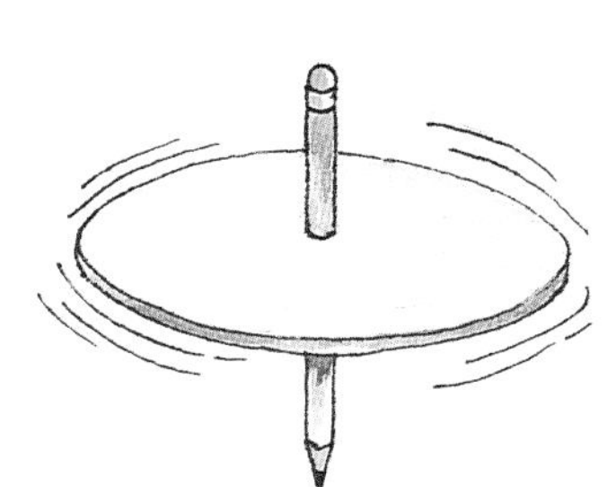

• To the Parent

Light refracts, or bends, when it passes from one medium to another. Sunlight is made up of seven colours, each of which has a different wavelength. When sunlight passes through a prism the light separates into its constituent colours with the shorter wavelengths refracting at greater angles than the longer wavelengths. Since violet light has the shortest wavelength it bends the most; red light has the longest wavelength, so it bends the least.

Why Is Some Smoke Black While Other Smoke Is Grey or White?

ANSWER It depends on how well things burn. Things that burn well give off white smoke. White smoke contains water vapour and carbon dioxide. Things that do not burn as well give off black smoke. This smoke has soot in it. Smoke that is grey has ashes in it.

▲ Factory chimneys make a lot of smoke.

Blue smoke

Smoke sometimes looks blue instead of white. Sunlight, you will remember, is made up of seven colours. When sunlight hits moisture in smoke, the blue light scatters. This usually happens when the sky is quite dark, like at dusk.

A Lack of Oxygen Makes Smoke Black

Things need oxygen to burn. This usually comes from the air. When a fire gets enough oxygen nearly everything burns up. But if there is not enough oxygen things do not burn as much. The unburnt bits become soot and make smoke black.

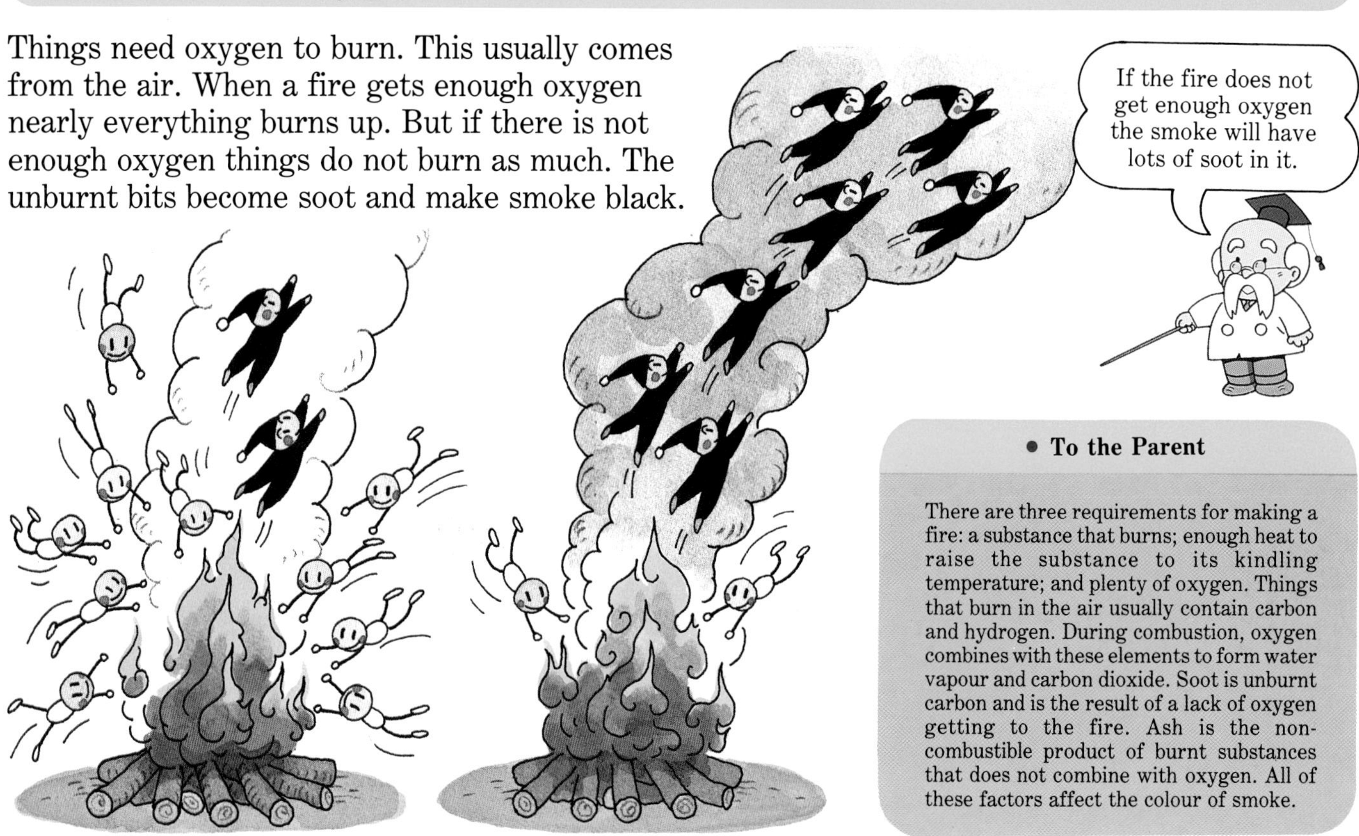

• To the Parent

There are three requirements for making a fire: a substance that burns; enough heat to raise the substance to its kindling temperature; and plenty of oxygen. Things that burn in the air usually contain carbon and hydrogen. During combustion, oxygen combines with these elements to form water vapour and carbon dioxide. Soot is unburnt carbon and is the result of a lack of oxygen getting to the fire. Ash is the non-combustible product of burnt substances that does not combine with oxygen. All of these factors affect the colour of smoke.

Why Can't We See Smells?

ANSWER Something smells when bits of it, called molecules, float in the air. Molecules are much too small to see. When they enter your nose, nerves send a message to your brain. When that happens, you smell something.

▲ Flowers have a very nice smell.

What Is the Difference between a Pleasant Smell and an Unpleasant Smell?

A pleasant smell makes us feel good, but a bad smell bothers us. Although we may not like bad smells, sometimes they help us. For instance, a bad smell can warn us that food has spoilt.

We usually think that flowers smell nice and spoilt food smells bad.

A smell that is pleasant to one person may not be pleasant to somebody else. Food that we like smells good to us, but food that we don't like does not.

Whether certain things smell good or bad depends on our own tastes.

Musk is one of the things perfume is made of. It comes from the musk deer. Straight from the deer, musk has a strong, unpleasant smell. But if the musk is thinned with alcohol the smell becomes a nice one. Too many molecules entering our nose from something we usually like can make it smell bad.

Natural musk is too strong. Diluted musk smells good.

The musk deer lives in mountain ranges in Asia. We get musk only from the male deer.

• To the Parent

Many different substances release molecules into the air. Smell is the detection of these molecules by receptor cells that are located on a mucous lining inside the nasal cavity. The receptor cells are part of the olfactory nerves and when molecules become attached to the mucous lining they can stimulate the receptor cells to transmit impulses along the olfactory nerves to the olfactory centre in the brain. The brain interprets the impulses as information about the smell.

Why Does a Golf Ball Have Dimples?

ANSWER The small hollows on the surface of a golf ball are called dimples. They make the ball travel much farther through the air. They also help make shots more accurate.

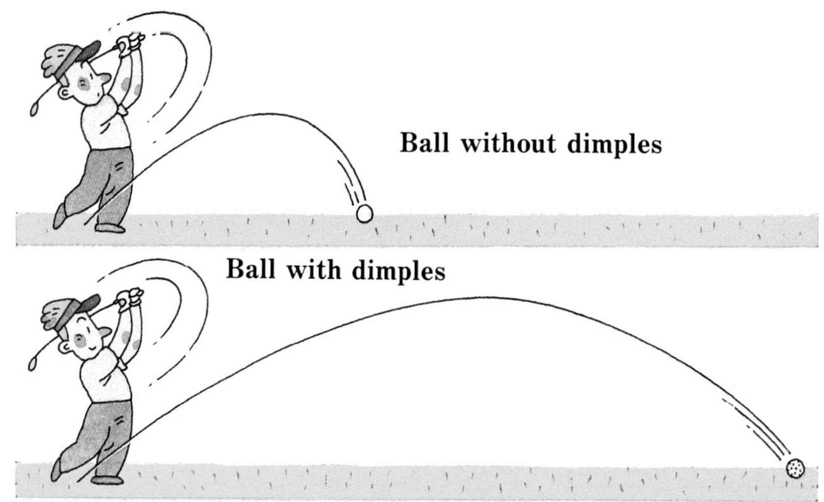

■ Inside a golf ball

In the centre of a golf ball is a small rubber sac filled with liquid. Tightly wrapped around this is rubber thread. On top of that is a thin rubber-like cover with dimples in it. The depth and arrangement of the dimples vary with different kinds of balls. These factors can affect how far and high the balls will go.

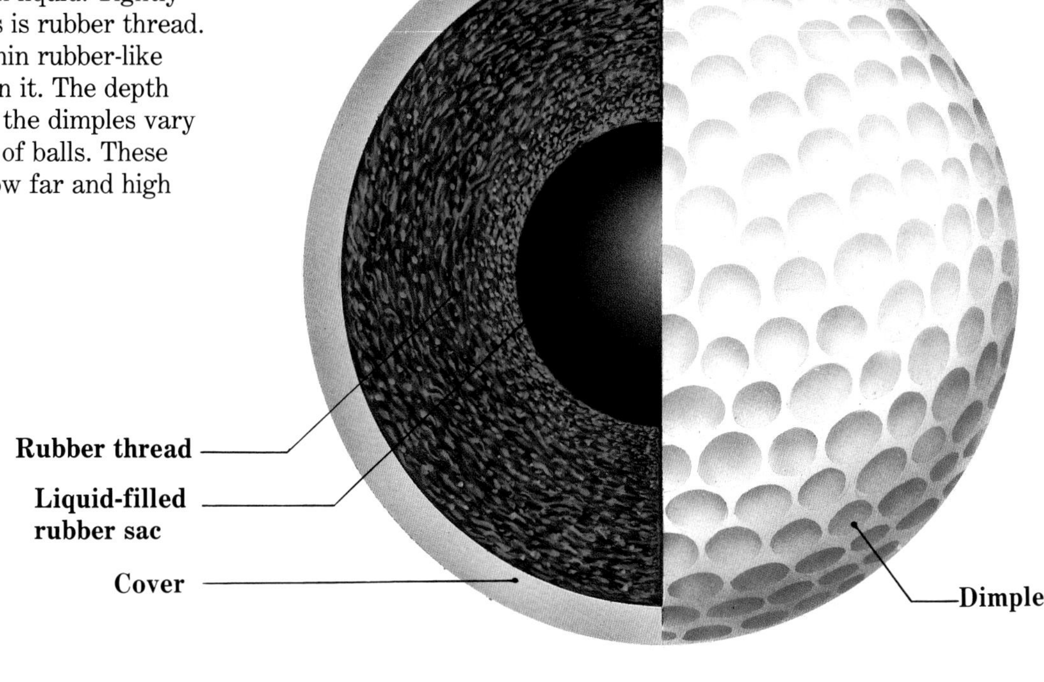

Why Does a Ball with Dimples Go Farther?

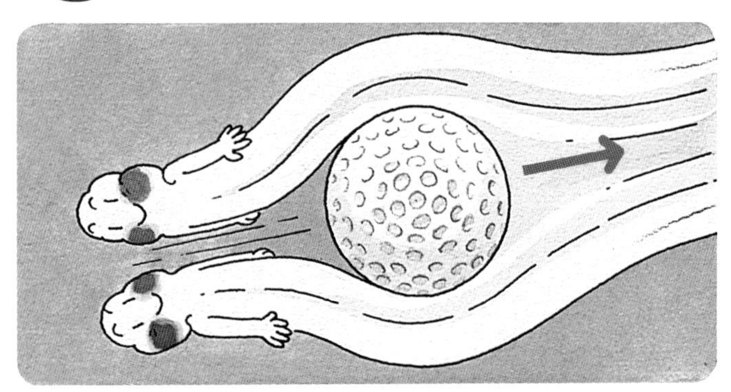

A golf ball forces air out of its way as it moves. The dimples help the air move quickly behind the ball, so it travels farther.

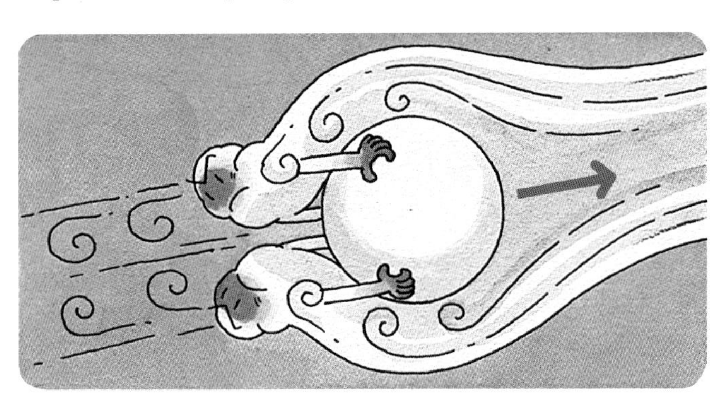

With no dimples the air does not move behind the ball as fast, so the ball does not go as far.

Golfers also use different types of clubs to make the ball go farther or higher.

• To the Parent

Golf developed in Scotland from a Roman game called *paganica*, in which players used a bent stick to hit a soft ball. Early golfers used wooden balls, but these were superseded in the early 17th century by stitched leather balls stuffed with boiled feathers. These gave way to balls made from gutta-percha in about 1842. The rubber ball, shown above, was introduced in the early 20th century. It greatly increased golf's popularity because it is easier to hit into the air and goes much farther than the gutta-percha ball.

Why Does a Tennis Ball Curve If It Is Hit with a Sliced Shot?

ANSWER If you hit a tennis ball with a slicing action it makes the ball spin. The spin makes the ball curve through the air. If you are right-handed the ball curves to the left. If you are left-handed it curves to the right.

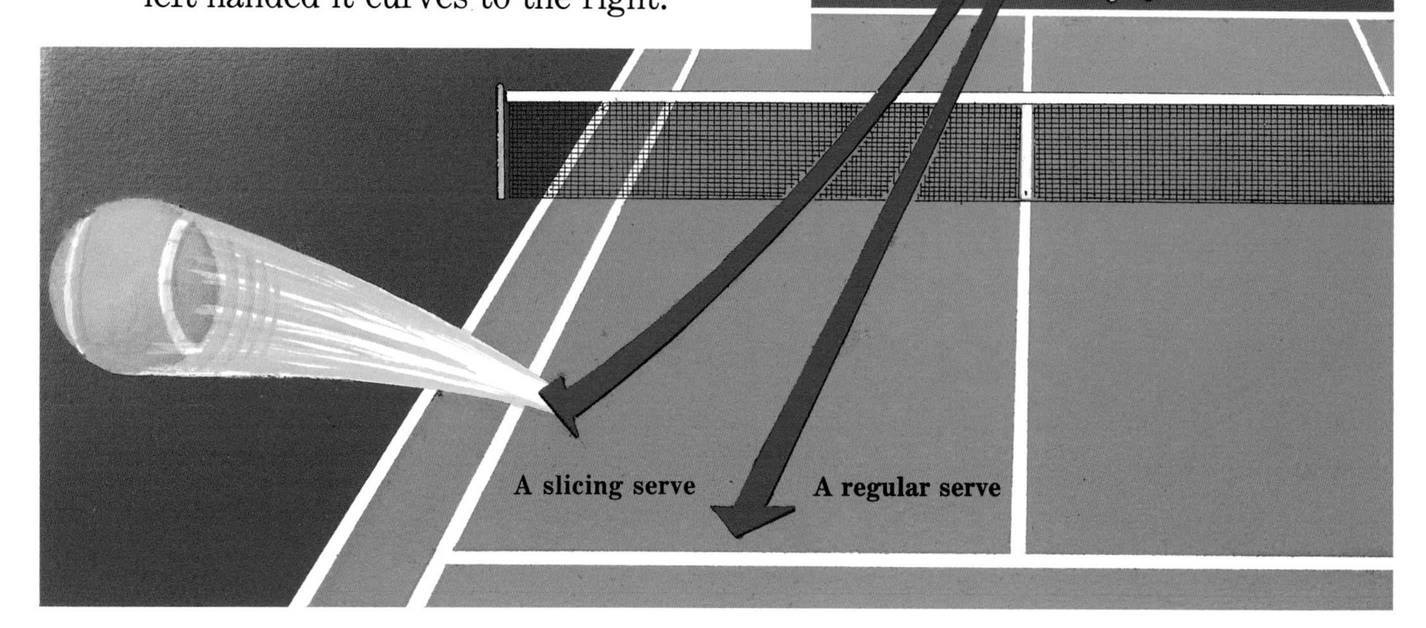

How to make a sliced shot

Swing the racket downward onto the back of the ball. Continue to bring the racket head down through the ball and then bring it up to finish the swing.

Why the ball curves

A spinning ball causes the air to flow faster on one side. The ball is pulled toward the faster air and it curves.

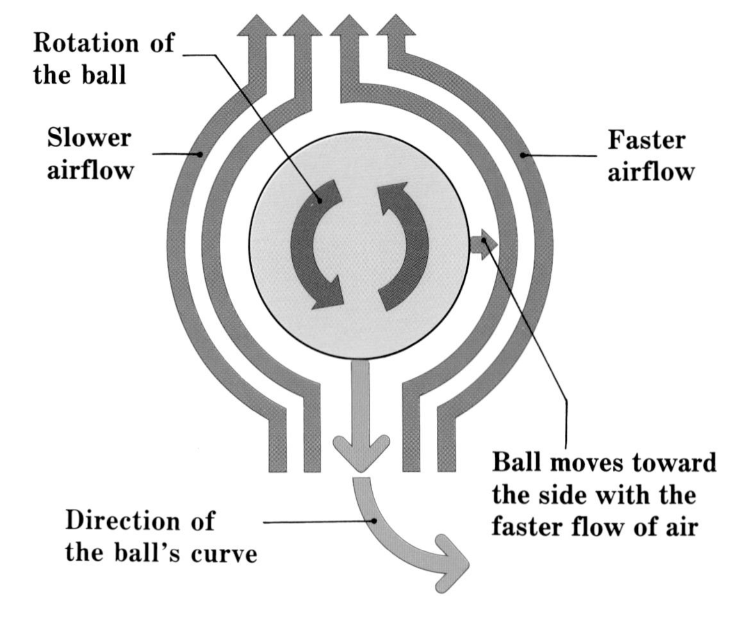

Why Does Hitting the Ball with Topspin Make It Fall So Fast?

Giving a ball topspin makes the air move faster below it than above. The ball is pulled toward the faster air and so drops quickly.

Topspin shot

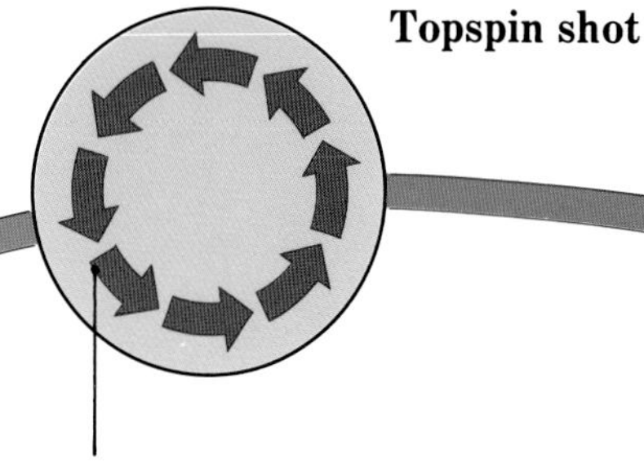

The ball spins quickly.

In a regular shot the ball spins less quickly. There is not as much downward pull, so the ball does not fall as fast.

Regular shot

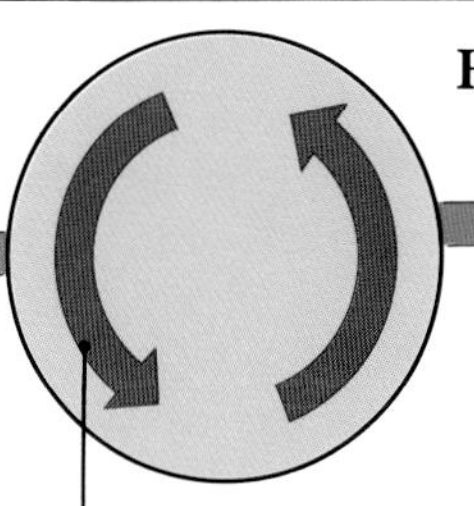

The ball rotates more slowly with a regular shot.

■ How to give a ball topspin

To give the ball topspin, bring the racket up to meet the ball from below. Then brush the back of the ball with the racket's face and sweep over it.

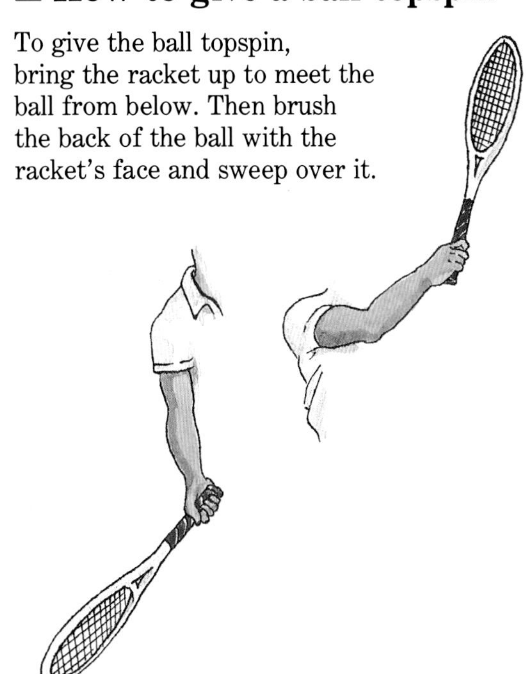

■ Why does the ball fall so fast?

The ball moves toward the faster airflow. Since this is below it, the ball moves downward and falls quickly.

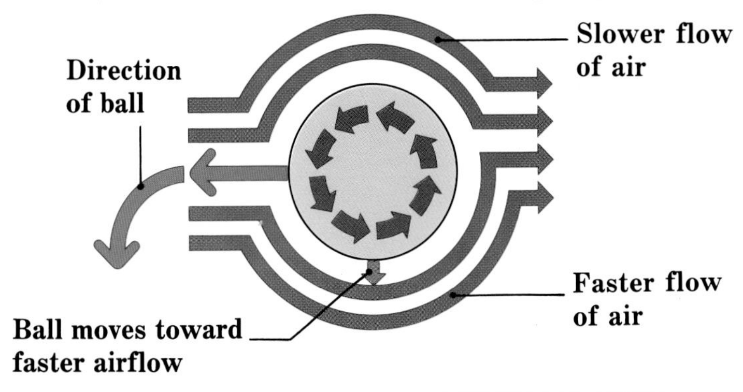

• To the Parent

A slice from a right-handed person makes a tennis ball spin and curve to the left from the player's perspective. The spin increases the speed of air flowing around the ball's left side. This faster airflow decreases the air pressure and pulls the ball to the left. For a similar reason, a ball with topspin falls faster than one without.

How Do Fishermen Find Fish in the Oceans?

ANSWER 1 Sometimes fishermen use a special device called a fishfinder. The fishfinder sends out sound waves. The sound waves bounce off schools of fish and are reflected back to the fishfinder. They appear on the fishfinder's screen and show fishermen where the fish are.

This fishfinder uses colours to show where fish are. Red shows where there are many fish and yellow shows where there are some.

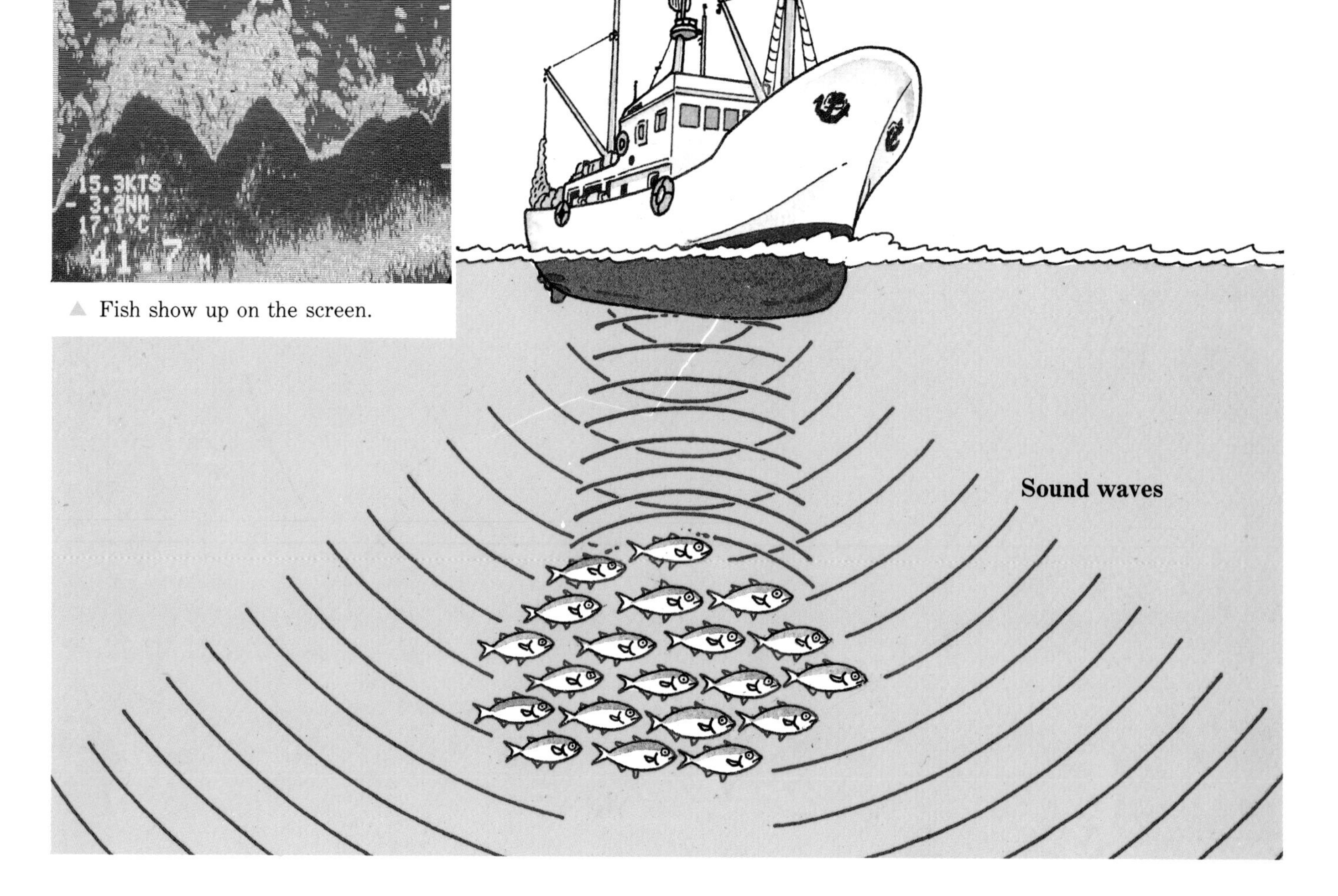

Fish show up on the screen.

ANSWER 2 They can use satellite information, too. Fish like to swim in areas of the ocean where the temperature suits them. Fishermen know what temperatures fish like. Some satellites can read ocean temperatures. Using the satellite information fishermen know where schools of fish are likely to be.

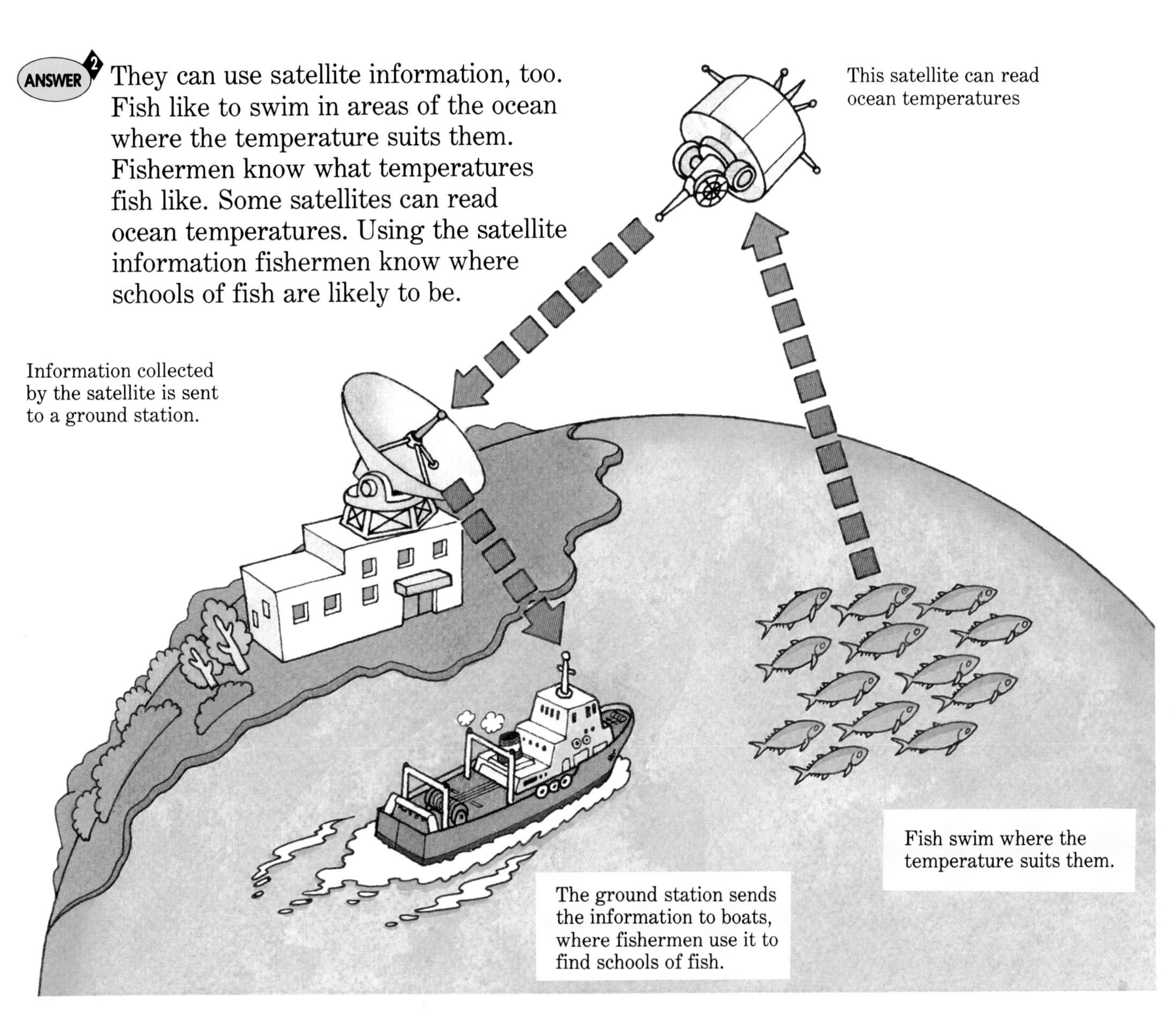

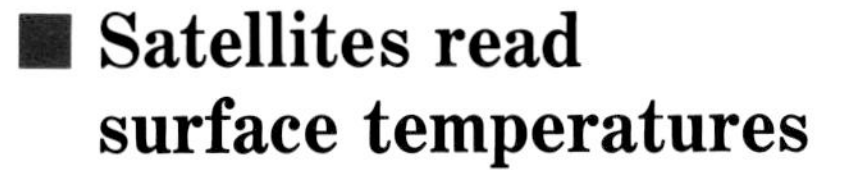

■ Satellites read surface temperatures

A satellite can detect only surface temperatures. So it can only help fishermen find schools of fish that swim near the surface of the oceans.

A satellite can help fishermen locate fish near the surface.

• To the Parent

A fishfinder operates in a similar way to radar except that a radar set uses radio waves, while a fishfinder employs high-frequency sound waves. The waves are emitted from a fishing boat and are reflected back when they hit objects, such as schools of fish, under the sea. There are two types of fishfinders. The simpler kind transmits sound waves downward and indicates the depths of the schools of fish it locates. The more complex kind transmits waves in all directions and provides more data on where schools are.

Why Don't Birds Get Shocked When They Sit on an Electric Wire?

ANSWER When electricity passes through the body of a person or an animal it causes an electric shock. But when a bird is perched on an electric wire the electricity passes through the wire not through the bird. That is why the bird does not get shocked.

Electric wires come from a power station

Electricity comes from power stations. It passes along wires from the power stations to our offices, factories and homes. The force pushing the electricity through the wires is called voltage. The voltage is very high when the electricity leaves a power station. To make the electricity safe for people to use, transformers and substations lower the voltage. In some places underground cables carry the electricity instead of overhead wires.

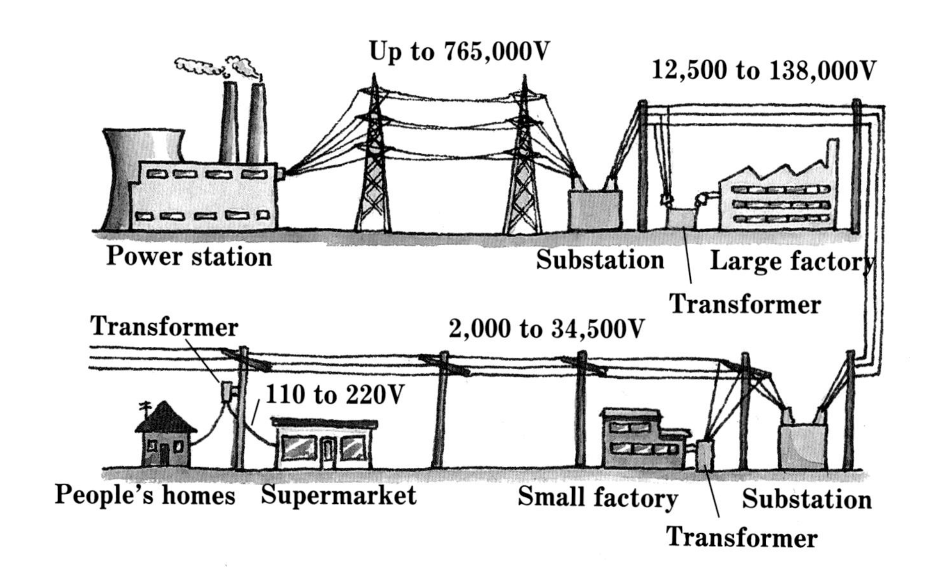

Why some birds are killed by wires

Electricity flows between two different voltages. If a bird perches on two wires, or if its body touches an electric pole when it is on a wire, it makes a path for electricity to flow between two different voltages.

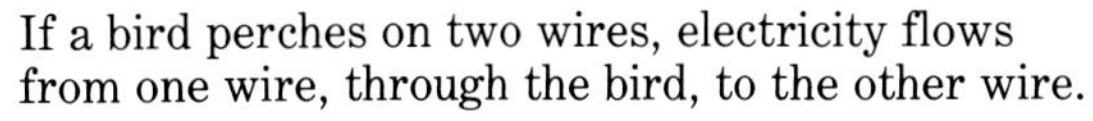

If a bird perches on two wires, electricity flows from one wire, through the bird, to the other wire.

If a bird touches an electric pole, electricity flows through the bird and the pole to the ground.

How Does an Electric Shock Kill a Bird?

When electricity passes through something, heat is produced. When a strong electric current flows through a bird or other animal it makes enough heat to cause a bad burn. The shock caused by the current can make the animal's heart stop. Even low-voltage electricity can kill animals and people.

• To the Parent

Most electric power stations burn fossil fuels to drive generators, which create an electromotive force, or voltage, that pushes an electric current through wires. The wires distribute the electric current to homes, offices and factories. Since electric currents will flow between voltage differences, people or animals forming a bridge between an electric wire and another medium will become part of an electric circuit and electricity will flow through them.

Why Does Food Spoil?

ANSWER When food gets old it spoils. That happens because there are bacteria in food. Bacteria are so tiny that you cannot see them. Over time the bacteria grow in number. They change proteins and other substances in food. When they do that we say the food is spoilt.

When bacteria attack food, the food changes colour and shape. It can smell bad too.

The food spoilers

Bacteria live by changing substances.

Food changed by bacteria can no longer be eaten.

Why Does Spoilt Food Make Us Feel Ill If We Eat It?

Over time the number of bacteria in food rises. Eating food with a lot of bacteria in it can give us a stomachache. Also, as bacteria break down food they can produce harmful substances. These substances can make us feel ill.

Be sure not to eat food that has spoilt.

You can get a stomachache if you eat food with lots of bacteria in it.

Some bacteria produce harmful substances that make you feel sick.

Some Bacteria Are Useful

Bacteria change substances into other things. These changes can be useful to us. For example, bacteria break down the ingredients of milk to make yoghurt and cheese. And when bacteria break down alchohol they make vinegar.

Two kinds of bacteria break down milk to make yoghurt. Bacteria and oxygen in the air turn alcohol into vinegar.

Like yoghurt, cheese starts with milk. Bacteria help break down the milk to make cheese.

• To the Parent

Bacteria are unicellular microorganisms that occur nearly everywhere. Although most bacteria are harmless to people, the build-up of certain varieties, like *Salmonella,* in food can lead to food poisoning. The toxic secretions of bacteria, such as botulin from *Clostridium botulinum,* can also lead to food poisoning. Beneficial effects of bacterial action include breaking down organic waste, producing antibiotics and making various foods.

Did You Know That Diamonds Are the Hardest Stones?

ANSWER Diamonds are made of carbon. The tiniest bits of carbon are called atoms. The way the carbon atoms fit together in a diamond makes this stone very hard.

This man is digging for diamonds.

A diamond that is surrounded by rock.

The diamond after it has been taken out of the rock.

• To the Parent

A diamond is the hardest naturally occurring substance, but graphite, which is also composed of carbon atoms, is quite soft. Though both are crystalline in structure, the difference between them arises from the way the atoms are arranged. Diamonds form only when carbon is exposed to intense heat and pressure in the upper mantle. They are mined primarily from a rock known as kimberlite, which geologists believe rose rapidly to the surface in volcanic eruptions aeons ago.

Diamond and graphite are related

Diamond and graphite are both made of carbon atoms. But the atoms are arranged differently in graphite.

Cutting diamonds

Diamonds are so hard that only other diamonds will cut them. A round saw with diamond dust around its edge is used.

This machine cuts and polishes diamonds.

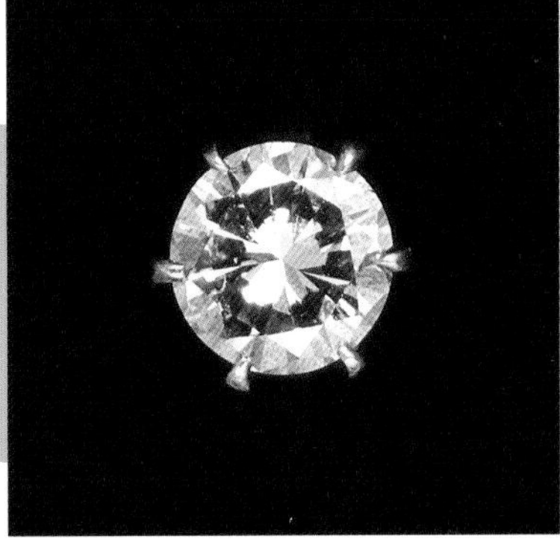

A cut and polished diamond set in a ring.

Why Doesn't the World Run Out of Oxygen?

ANSWER People and animals breathe in oxygen and breathe out carbon dioxide. But green plants take in carbon dioxide and give off oxygen. So, as long as there are plenty of green plants, like grass and trees, the world will not run out of oxygen.

Nature's Balance

People and animals breathe in air to supply their bodies with oxygen. They breathe out lots of carbon dioxide.

Plants take in carbon dioxide and give off oxygen. That is why we do not run short of oxygen.

Photosynthesis

Green plants make their own food. They take carbon dioxide from the air and water from the soil. In the leaves is a green substance called chlorophyll. Chlorophyll uses sunlight as energy to change the carbon dioxide and water into plant food. This process is called photosynthesis. Oxygen is released during photosynthesis.

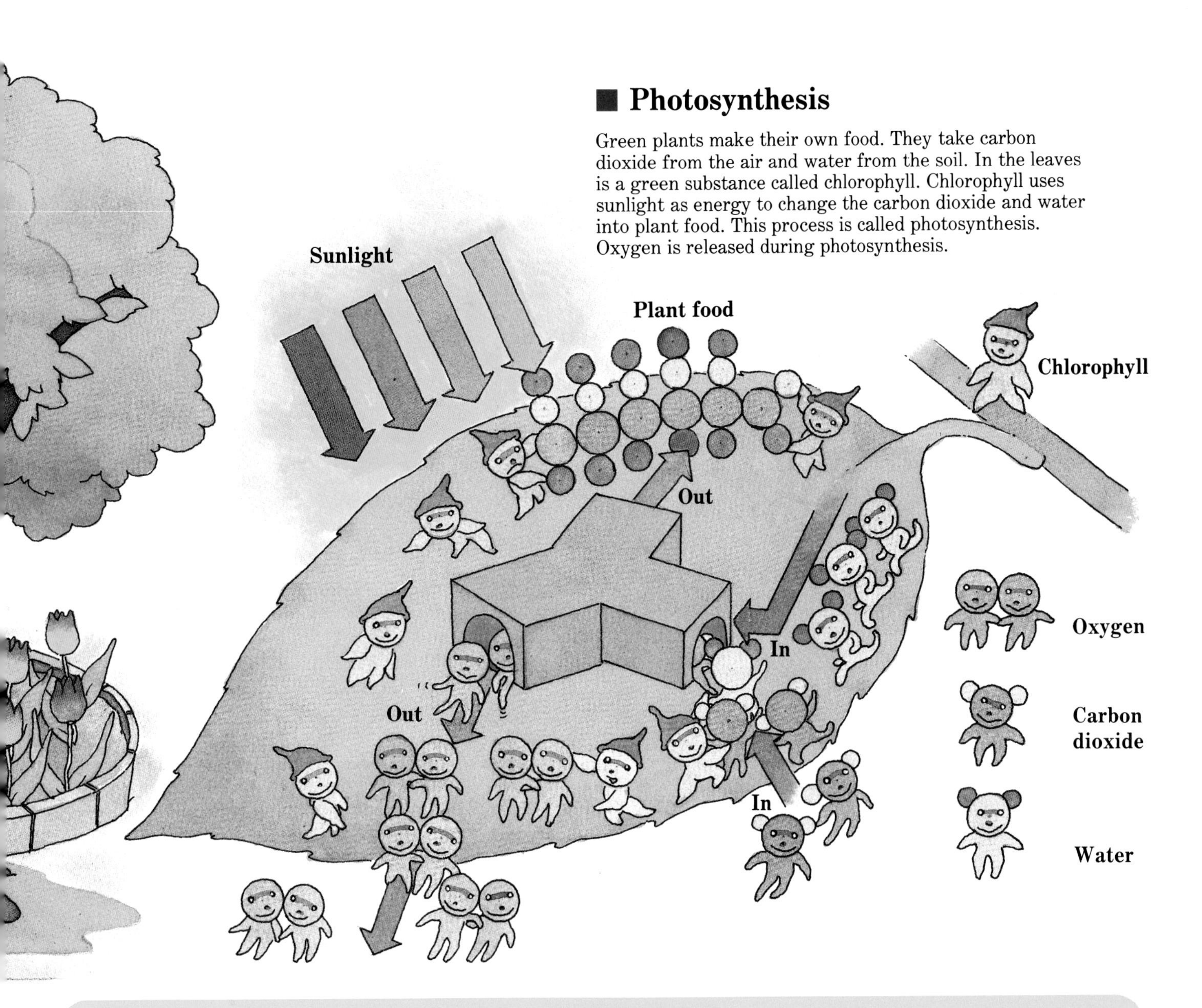

Will We Ever Run Short of Oxygen?

If more and more forests are cut down, it could lower the supply of oxygen.

• To the Parent

Green plants make their own food through the process of photosynthesis, during which chlorophyll uses sunlight as energy to convert carbon dioxide and water into glucose; oxygen is released as a by-product. Cellular respiration is the process that converts food into a usable energy source. It takes place in the cells of humans, animals and most plants. It requires oxygen and releases carbon dioxide and water as by-products. It is thought that over 75 percent of photosynthesis occurs in the oceans in phytoplankton. But incessant deforestation could still affect the world's oxygen supply.

Why Does Ice Float?

ANSWER Like most substances, water is made up of many small particles called molecules. In water the molecules are packed tightly together. The molecules in ice are not packed together so tightly. This makes ice lighter than water, so it floats.

Ice is lighter than water, but not much. About one-eighth of an iceberg shows above the surface of the sea.

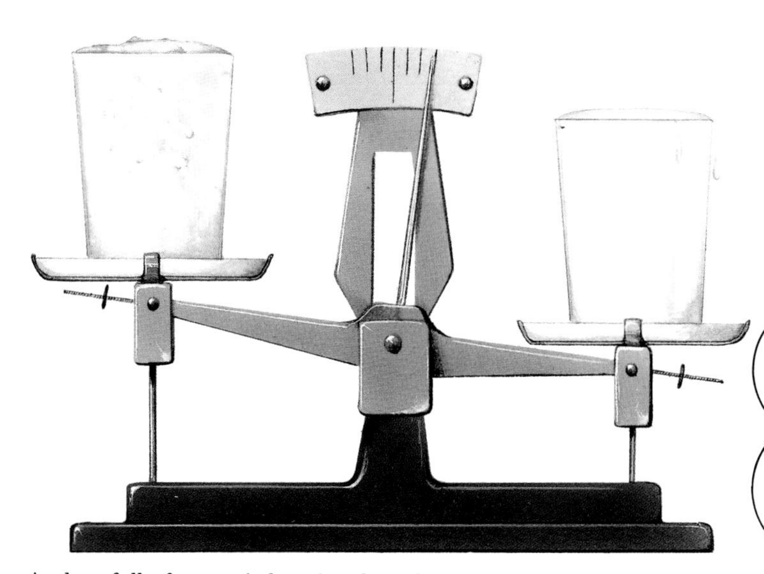

A glass full of water is heavier than the same glass full of ice.

Everything is made up of tiny particles called atoms. Often the bonds between two or more atoms are so strong that the atoms join together to form another particle called a molecule. Molecules of water contain two hydrogen atoms and one oxygen atom.

Molecules in water and ice

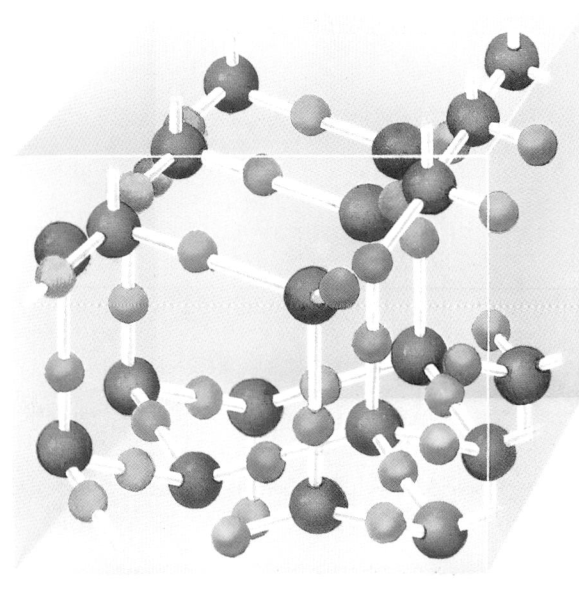

If ice turns to water the gaps will become much smaller.

If the water turns to ice the gaps will grow larger.

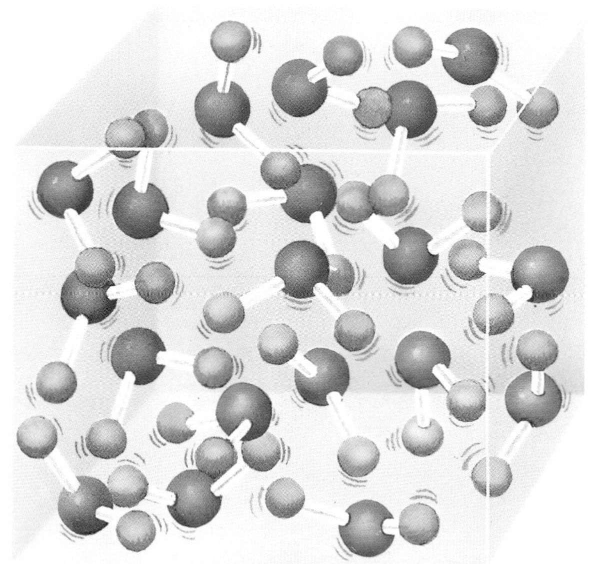

The gaps between molecules in ice are wider.

The molecules in water are packed more tightly.

TRY THIS

Put ice into a glass and then fill the glass with water. You can see that the ice rises above the top of the glass. Do you think that the water will overflow when the ice melts? It will not because the number of molecules remains the same.

Fill the glass with water and freeze it. When all the water has frozen you will see that the ice rises above the top of the glass. That happens because water expands when it freezes. When water turns into ice, its volume increases by about 9 percent.

Did You Know That a Lake Freezes from the Top?

When water cools to below 39° Fahrenheit (4° C.) the molecules begin to spread out, making the water lighter. This lighter water rises to the top of a lake where cold air freezes it. Ice floats on a lake's surface because it is lighter than the water below.

The top is frozen.

The water here is still not frozen.

• To the Parent

Water is the only substance that appears in solid, liquid and gaseous states in the world's natural range of temperatures. Water is at its densest at 39° Fahrenheit (4° C.). Below this temperature the liquid expands and its density decreases. This explains why lighter, colder water rises to the surface of lakes where it is frozen by cold air. Water molecules fit more closely together when they are loosely linked, as in a liquid, than when their bonds are stronger, as in ice. Consequently ice floats.

Why Doesn't Dry Ice Turn to Water the Way Regular Ice Does?

ANSWER Regular ice is solid water. When it melts it turns into liquid water. But dry ice is not made from water. Instead it is the solid state of carbon dioxide. Carbon dioxide is a gas in the air around us. When dry ice melts it turns into carbon dioxide gas.

How the Molecules in Water and Carbon Dioxide Behave

If we heat water to 212° Fahrenheit (100° C.) the bonds between its molecules break. The molecules fly off in all directions and water becomes a gas. When water gets cold the bonds between its molecules get stronger. At 32° Fahrenheit (0° C.), the bonds are so strong that water turns into ice.

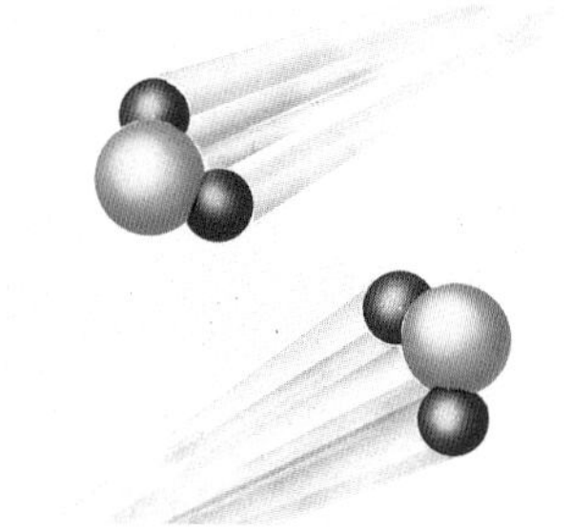

Water molecules as gas

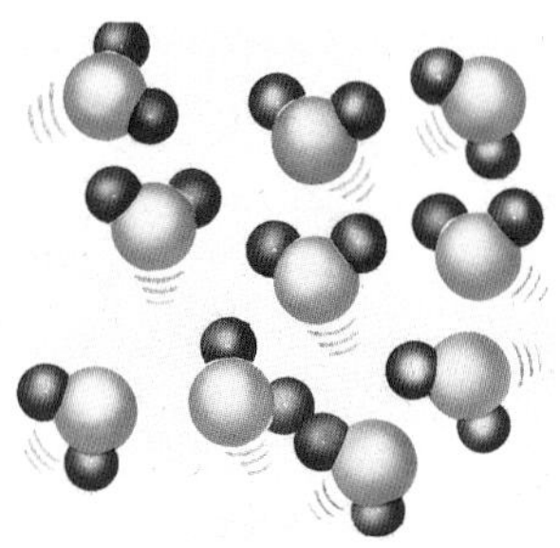

Water molecules as liquid

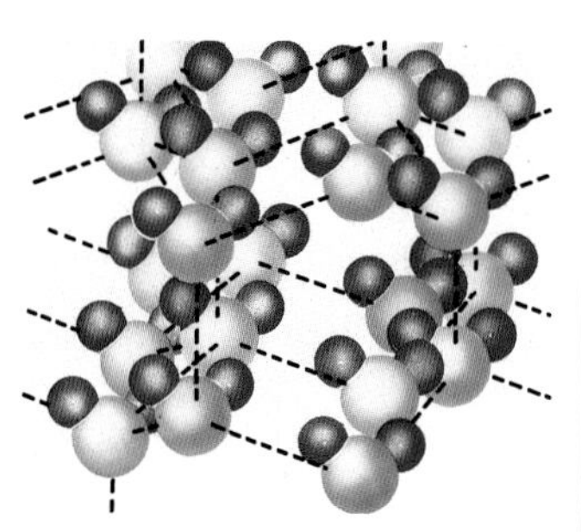

Water molecules as ice

Carbon dioxide is usually a gas in the air around us. But if it is cooled to -109.3° Fahrenheit (-78.5° C.), it becomes a solid without turning into a liquid first. The pressure must be much higher than normal for carbon dioxide to turn into a liquid.

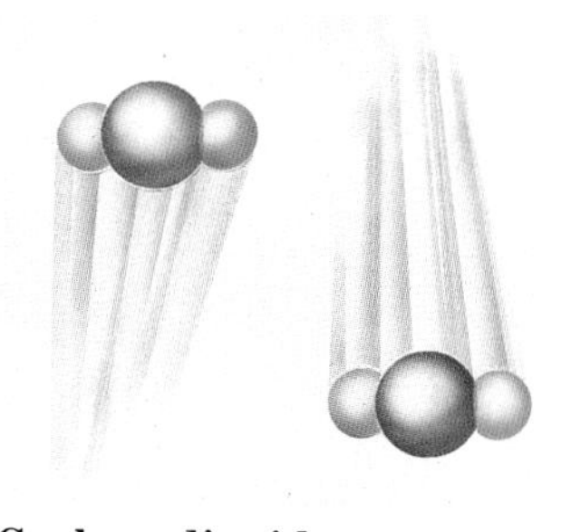

Carbon dioxide as gas

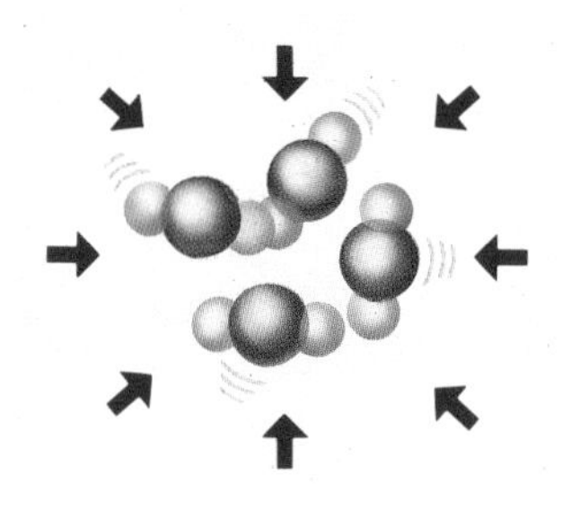

Carbon dioxide as liquid

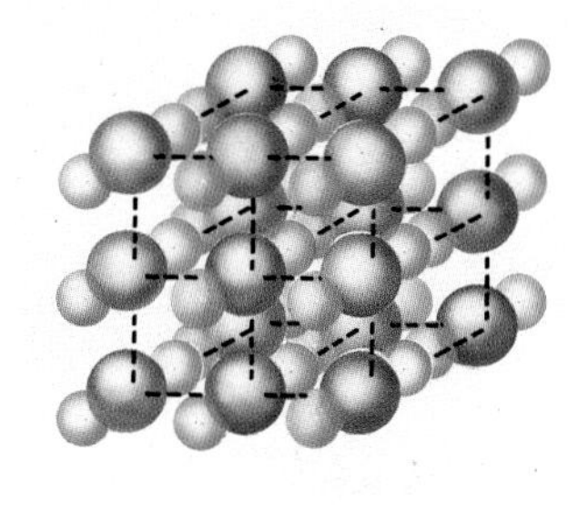

Carbon dioxide as dry ice

How Is Dry Ice Made?

To make dry ice, carbon dioxide is first put under very high pressure and cooled to -71° Fahrenheit (-57° C.). This turns it into a liquid. Then the pressure is suddenly reduced to normal air pressure. Instantly the liquid expands, which causes a sharp drop in temperature. This turns the carbon dioxide liquid into solid carbon dioxide. Dry ice looks like snow. It is pressed together to make blocks.

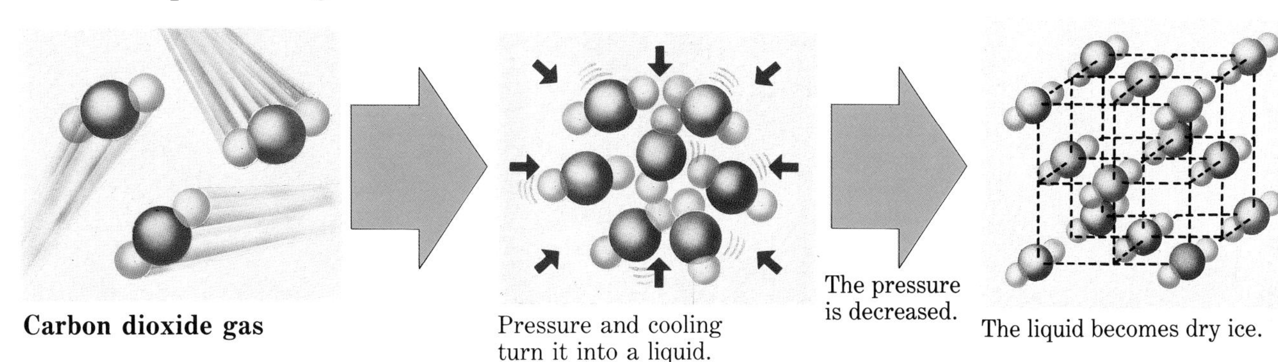

Carbon dioxide gas

Pressure and cooling turn it into a liquid.

The pressure is decreased.

The liquid becomes dry ice.

MINI-DATA

Water with dry ice in it bubbles as the carbon dioxide becomes a gas.

When dry ice is put into water with detergent in it, it makes soap bubbles of carbon dioxide.

Never touch dry ice with your bare hands. It is so cold that it will hurt you if you touch it.

• To the Parent

A combination of temperature and pressure determines what form a substance takes. At sea level, where atmospheric pressure is 14.72 pounds per square inch (1 at), water can be solid, liquid or gas depending on the temperature. Carbon dioxide, though, can exist only as a solid or gas at this pressure. To be a liquid the pressure must be increased to above 75.07 pounds per square inch (5.1 at). To make dry ice commercially the gas is liquified under pressure at -71° Fahrenheit (-57° C.) or lower. Then the pressure is suddenly decreased, which causes the liquid to expand rapidly before freezing into dry ice.

How Is Uranium Used to Make Electricity?

ANSWER Like all substances, uranium is made up of atoms. When uranium atoms are bombarded with tiny particles called neutrons they split apart. This causes them to release huge amounts of energy. Nuclear power stations change this energy into electricity.

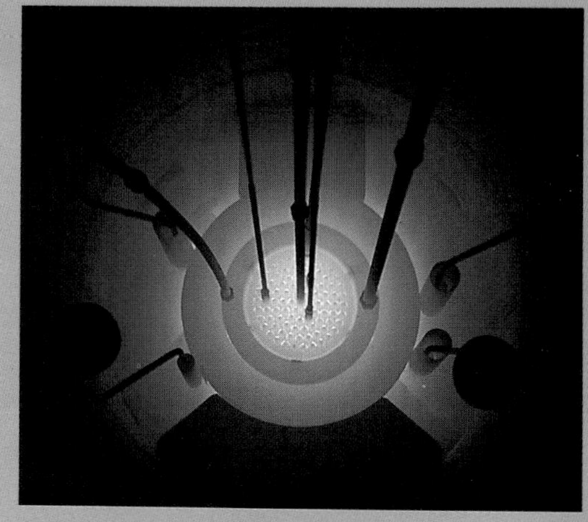

This is the reactor, where neutrons are fired at uranium atoms.

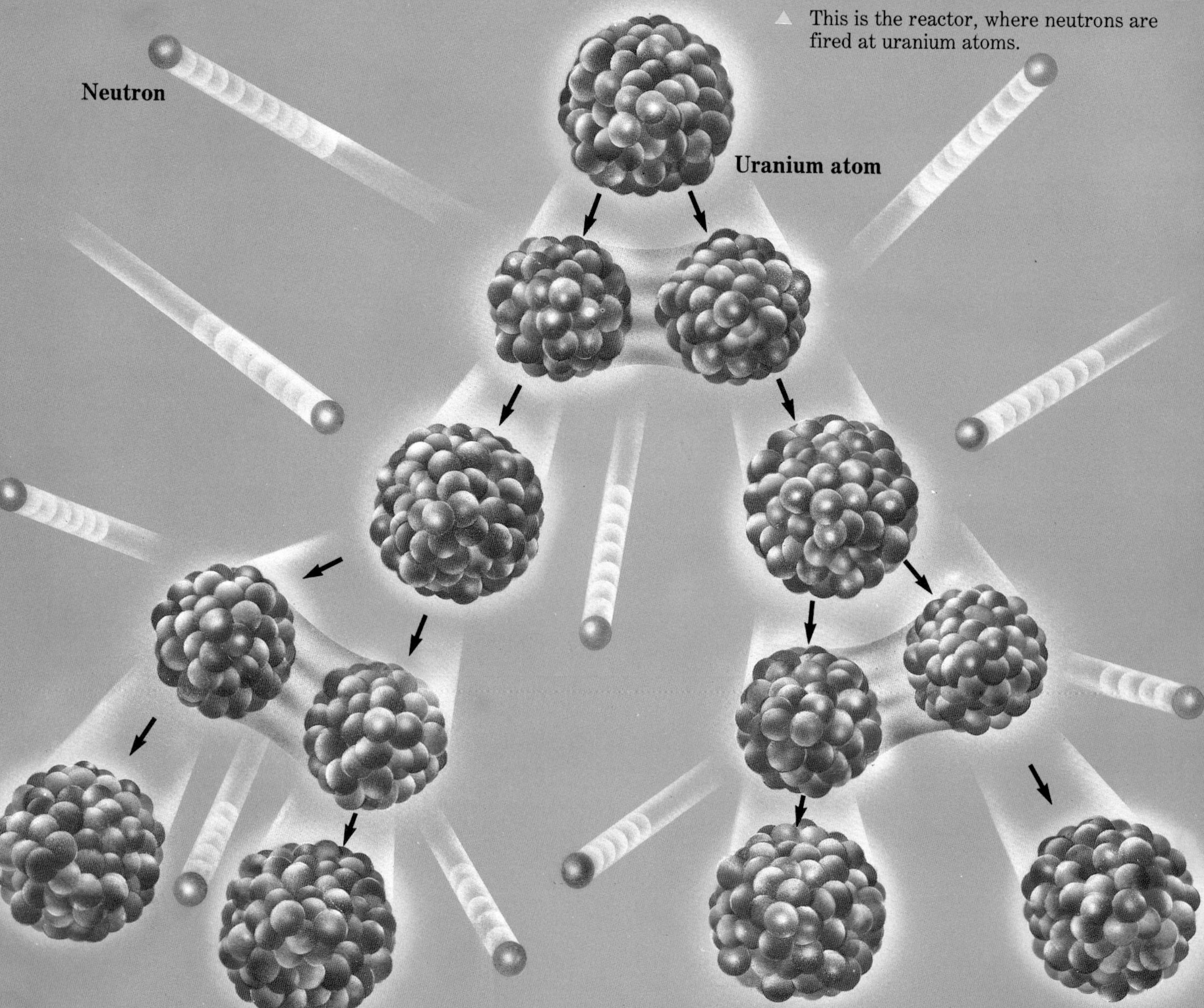

Inside a Nuclear Power Station

The place where uranium atoms are split is called a reactor. Heat created in the reactor from splitting atoms is used to boil water and produce steam. This steam then turns turbines to make electricity.

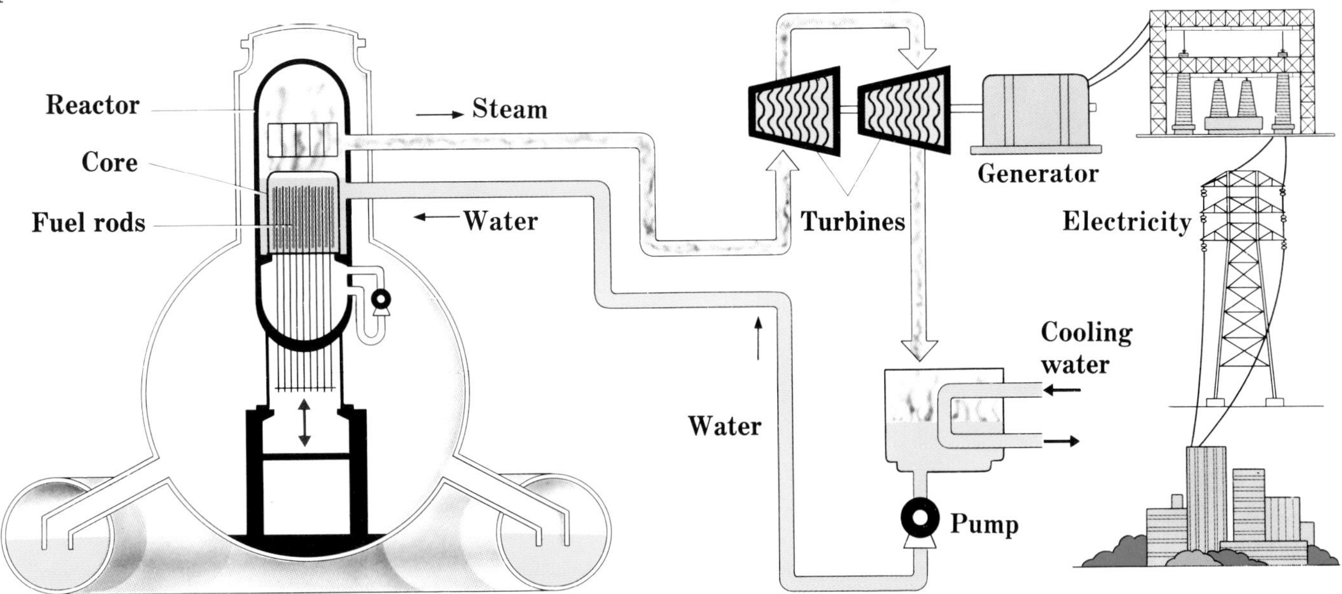

A Lot of Energy from a Little Fuel

Splitting the atoms of a tiny quantity of uranium creates as much energy as burning huge amounts of oil or coal.

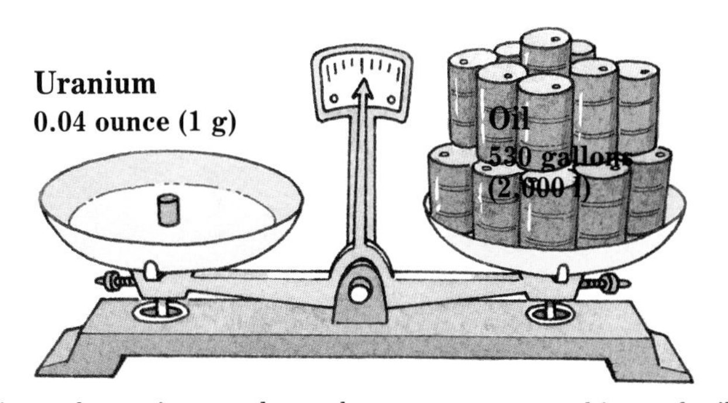

This much uranium produces the same energy as this much oil.

This much uranium produces the same energy as this much coal.

The energy from 0.04 ounce (1 g) of uranium can run 23,000 television sets for one hour. If you could use that energy to power a small car, you could travel halfway around the world.

• To the Parent

Splitting atoms to produce energy is called nuclear fission. Uranium-235, one of three isotopes, or forms, of the element, is used as fuel in nuclear reactors. Pellets of uranium-235 are put into stainless steel tubes to make fuel rods. Neutrons, which are particles in atomic nuclei, are fired at the rods. When a neutron strikes an atom of uranium the atom splits and releases two or three neutrons of its own. These can strike other atoms to start a chain reaction. The heat generated is used to produce electricity.

How Do Farmers Grow Seedless Grapes?

ANSWER Two weeks before flowers appear on grapevines, farmers dip the buds in a special liquid. This liquid contains a substance taken from fungi. Ten days after the flowers bloom farmers dip them again. This stops them from growing seeds.

Grape buds are dipped in this liquid.

Making seedless grapes

If farmers do not soak buds in the special solution, grapes with seeds will grow.

Grapes with seeds

If farmers soak the grape buds in the special solution, they will not grow seeds.

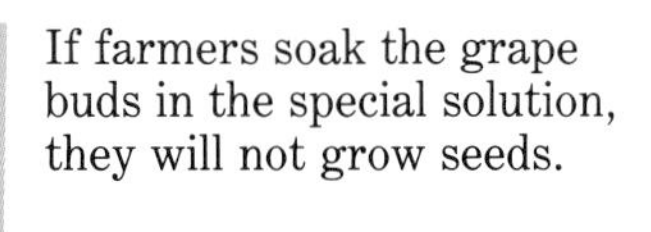

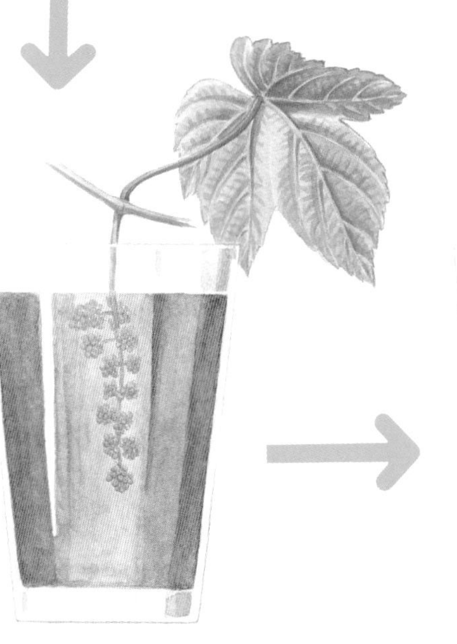

Buds are soaked before blooming.

They are soaked again after blooming.

Seedless grapes

Are Seedless Watermelons Grown the Same Way?

No. All living things have chromosomes in their cells. Chromosomes tell cells how to behave. Farmers make seedless watermelons by mixing watermelons that have different numbers of chromosomes.

Mixing a four-chromosome watermelon with a two-chromosome one makes a watermelon with three chromosomes. Mixing that with a two-chromosome watermelon makes a seedless watermelon.

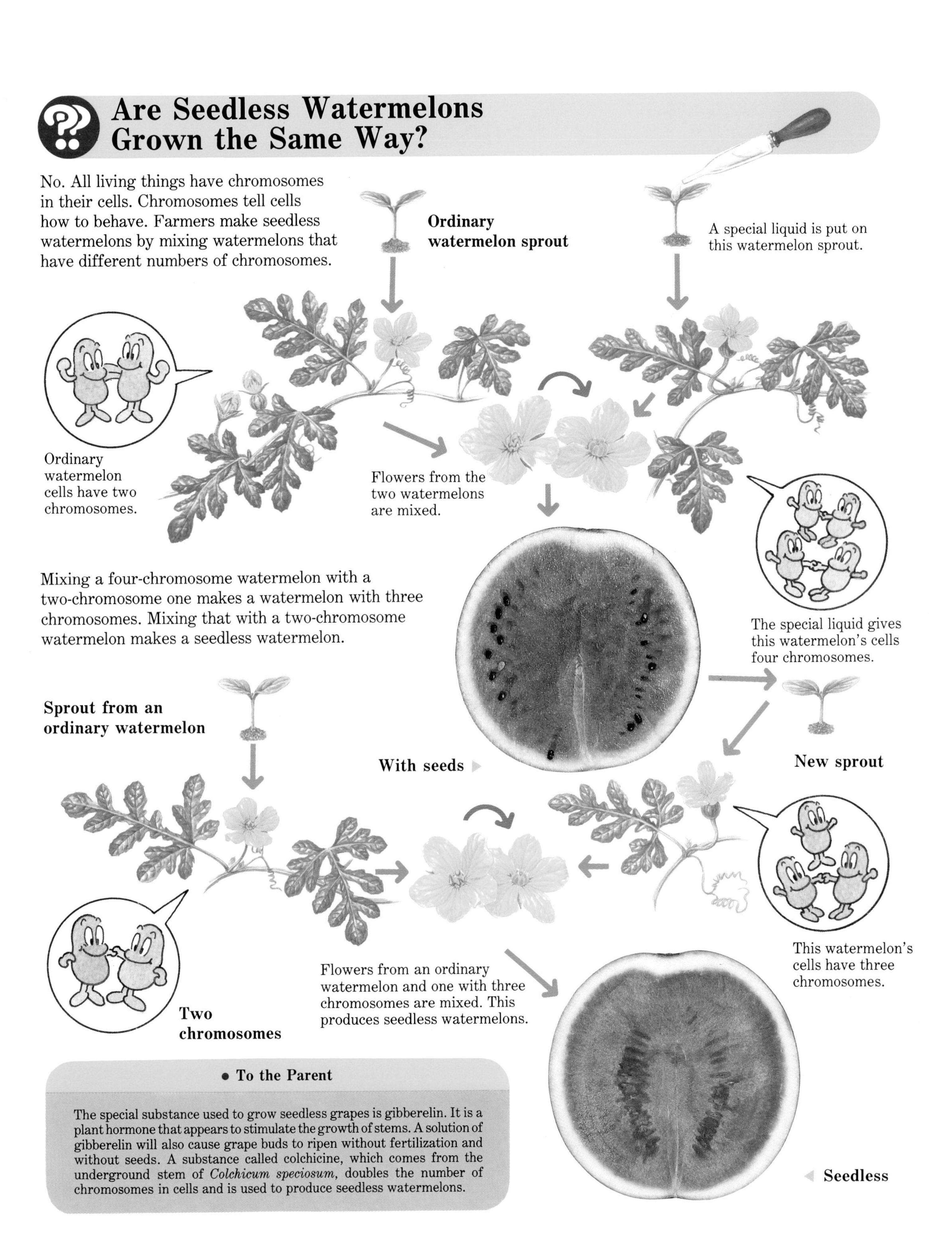

• To the Parent

The special substance used to grow seedless grapes is gibberelin. It is a plant hormone that appears to stimulate the growth of stems. A solution of gibberelin will also cause grape buds to ripen without fertilization and without seeds. A substance called colchicine, which comes from the underground stem of *Colchicum speciosum,* doubles the number of chromosomes in cells and is used to produce seedless watermelons.

How Is Glass Made?

ANSWER Glass is made from sand, lime and soda. When these ingredients are mixed up and heated they form liquid glass. In factories, liquid glass is made into sheets by cooling and flattening. To make it into pretty objects like vases, craftsmen blow into a glob of liquid glass on the end of a long tube.

▲ **Beautiful glasses**

■ Plate glass made by rolling

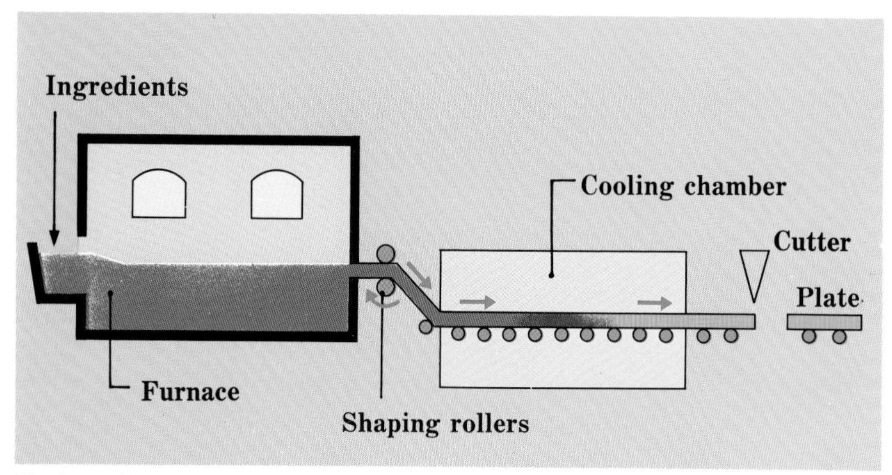

The ingredients are heated in a furnace to make liquid glass. Rollers flatten the glass into sheets, which are then cooled and cut.

▲ **Rolling process.** Rollers press the liquid glass into sheets to be cut.

■ Plate glass made by floating

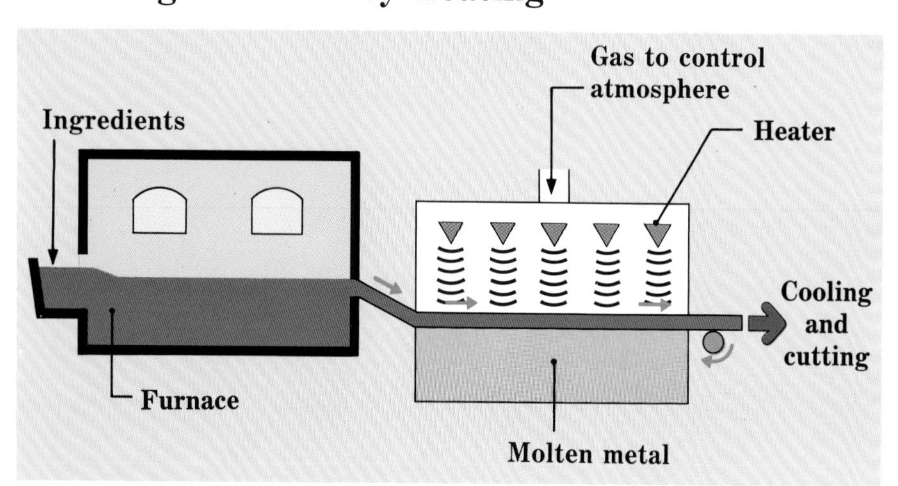

Liquid glass from a furnace is floated and slowly cooled on the surface of liquid tin. After the glass has cooled down it is cut into pieces.

▲ **Float-glass process.** Liquid glass cools as it floats on a bath of liquid tin.

Handmade Glassware

Vases, ornaments and other glass objects are made one at a time by glass-blowing. Using a metal blowpipe with a glob of hot glass at the end of it, a glass-blower blows the soft glass into shape.

▲ The ingredients are heated so that they turn into liquid glass.

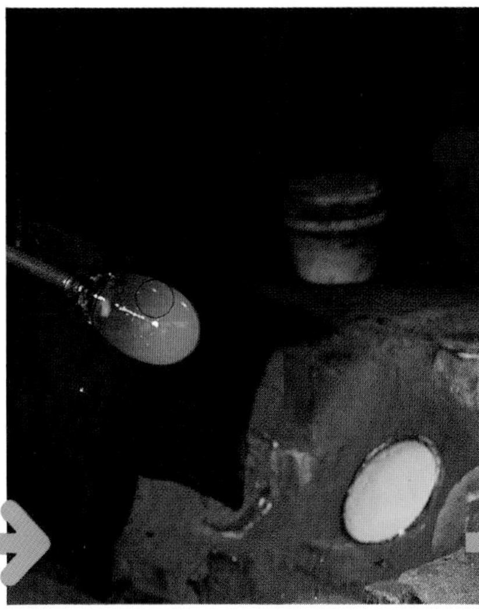

▲ A glob of melted glass is wound around the end of the blowpipe.

▲ The glass-blower turns the object to shape it while he blows.

Glass Has Many Uses

Window panes, mirrors and drinking glasses are just a few of the many things that are made of glass. Glass is not only useful, it can be beautiful too. Windows made of coloured, or stained, glass are works of art.

▲ **Stained-glass windows in a church**

• To the Parent

As well as silica, lime and soda, other glass-making ingredients may include alumina, lead oxide, saltpetre and zinc oxide to make different types of glass. In the production of plate glass, cullet—recycled or waste glass from a previous melt—is also added, making up 5 to 40 percent of the mixture. Melting occurs in giant furnaces from where molten glass is floated or rolled into sheets.

What Are These?

A waterfall

A waterfall is where water drops to a lower height. The highest waterfall in the world is Angel Falls in Venezuela. There the water falls 3,212 feet (979 m).

A U-shaped valley

This U-shaped valley was once V-shaped. U-shaped valleys were formed thousands of years ago by glaciers. Glaciers moved through V-shaped valleys and ground away their sides.

A karst

An area that has a lot of limestone in it is called a karst. Rainwater easily dissolves limestone, so karstic regions have caves, hollows and rocky surfaces, like the one shown here.

The sun's corona

The sun's corona is the outermost region of the sun's atmosphere. Usually we cannot see it because the sun's light is so bright. But if the moon passes between Earth and the sun to create an eclipse, we can see the corona around the edge of the moon.

An observatory

Inside an observatory is a large telescope. Astronomers use the telescope to observe stars and other objects in the sky. The dome of the observatory opens so that astronomers can look through the telescope at the sky. The telescope can be pointed in any direction.

Craters on the moon

These craters were formed by meteors that crashed into the moon. We do not see craters like this on Earth because meteors usually burn up before they reach the ground. This is because they hit air in Earth's atmosphere. The moon has no atmosphere, so meteors can crash into it at high speed.

• To the Parent

When rainwater mixes with carbon dioxide in the air or from the soil it becomes slightly acidic. It can then easily erode limestone areas to create rocky outcrops, sinkholes, troughs and underground caverns. Guilin in China is one area famous for its karst topography. It is only during a solar eclipse, when the moon prevents us from seeing the sun, that the corona becomes visible.

And What Are These?

The Milky Way

There are billions of galaxies in the universe. The Solar System is part of the galaxy called the Milky Way. The Milky Way is a spiralling cloud of billions of stars like our sun.

Magnetic lines of force

You cannot see them but there are magnetic force lines around magnets. You can see the effect of those force lines if you put a magnet on a piece of paper and sprinkle iron filings around it. The force lines make the tiny pieces of iron form curved patterns like the ones shown here.

An astronaut in orbit

A spacecraft and anything else in orbit are in a state of weightlessness. The astronaut shown here is orbiting Earth at the same speed as his nearby spacecraft. That is why he does not fall but instead stays close to the spacecraft.

• To the Parent

The Milky Way is a spiral galaxy that spins its way through the universe like an enormous Catherine wheel. A thick bulge of billions of old stars lies at its centre while two arms of younger stars, dust and gas wind around the bulge as the galaxy turns. The Solar System is located 30,000 light years away from the spiral's centre on the Orion arm of the galaxy. Although one of the larger galaxies in the universe, the Milky Way is just one of billions of galaxies that vary in size and shape.

Growing-Up Album

How Are They Related?

The boys and girls shown here are doing things or are involved in situations that are related somehow to the objects at the bottom of these two pages. Can you figure out what that relationship is? Think about it, then match the objects below with the boys' and girls' actions and situations above.

1. It's raining.

2. He's swimming underwater.

3. They're looking at the stars.

4. They're ice skating.

What is the connection?

These 10 objects have something to do with the situations and actions that you see in the pictures above. Think about how they're related.

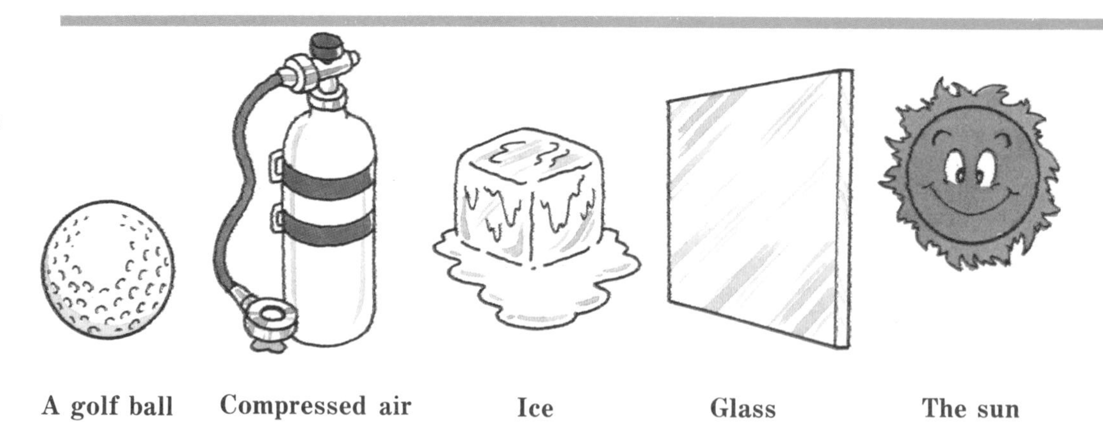

5. There are shadows on the ground.

6. They're figuring out which way to go.

7. She's playing golf.

8. He can see outside even though the window is closed.

9. She can eat her ice cream because it hasn't melted.

10. She's playing tennis.

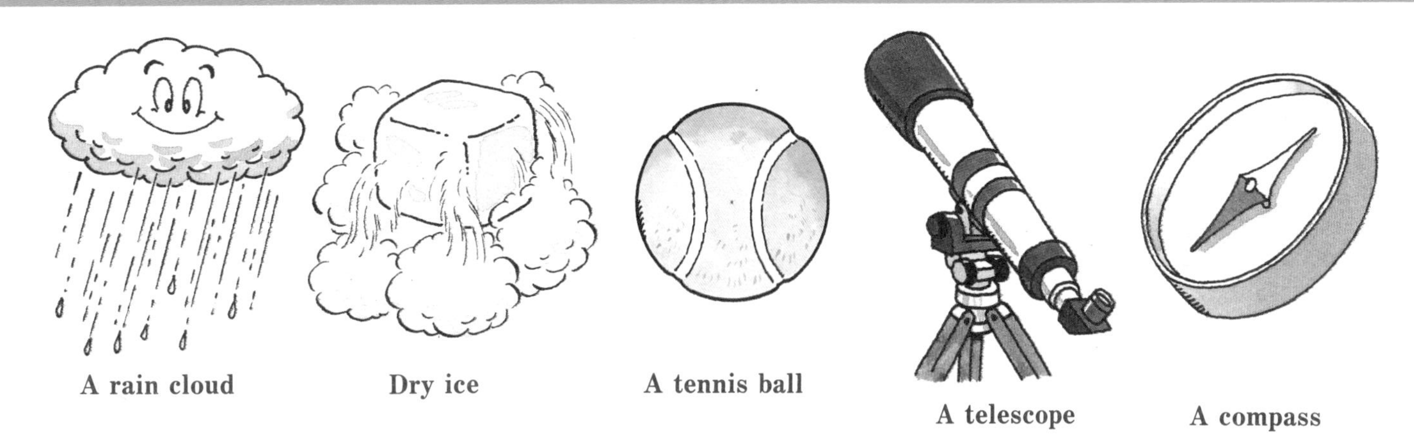

Answers 1—A rain cloud; 2—Compressed air; 3—A telescope; 4—Ice; 5—The sun; 6—A compass; 7—A golf ball; 8—Glass; 9—Dry ice; 10—A tennis ball

Which Shadows Match?

When the sun shines on a person or object it casts a shadow. In this picture you can see a lot of shadows. At the bottom are six more shadows. Look at them carefully, then match the shadows at the bottom with the people, animals or objects that made them.

■ Match the Shadows

These six shadows can be found in the picture above. Some of the shadows in the picture are similar, so look very carefully. For each one of these six shadows, there is only one exactly like it in the picture. Can you find it?

Answers 1—Light-coloured car on the right; 2—Dog in the park; 3—Boy next to trees in the park; 4—Boy on bicycle at bottom of picture; 5—Woman and baby in the park; 6—Tree at bottom of picture

How Do They Differ?

Water in rivers and the sea can differ in various ways. Study the large picture below and try to find the differences.

■ What are the differences?

Pictures 1 to 8 on the right show things that are related to rivers or the sea. Read the words below the pictures and look at the diagram above to help you figure out which things are related to rivers and which to the sea.

1. It can be held back by a dam.

2. It tastes salty.

3. It can create a waterfall.

4. Its current always flows the same way.

5. It sometimes has big waves.

6. It has a tide.

7. You can paddle a canoe here.

8. You can surf on it.

Answers 1, 3, 4, 7—Rivers; 2, 5, 6, 8—The sea

A Child's First Library of Learning

Science Starter

Adapted from Gakken's "Why? Why?"

Original English translation by:
International Editorial Services Inc.
Tokyo, Japan

English-language edition (Asia) published by:
Time Life Asia

President,
Time Life International: John D. Hall
VP Time Life International,
Managing Director, Asia: Trevor E. Lunn
CFO and General Manager: Norman Tsoi
Production Supervisor: Stephen Hon
Sales and Marketing
Director: Mushtaq A. Panjwani
New Product Development
Editorial Director: Kate Nussey
Senior Editor: Anne Tseng

New edition:
Project Manager: Kay Halsey
Project Editor: Andrew Bullard
Senior Editor: Katherine K. Rothschild
Publishing Coordinator: Hiroko Wilde

ISBN 0-8094-7287-2

First published 1989. New edition 1996
Reprinted 2002. Printed in China

Time Life Asia is a division of Time Life Inc.
An AOL Time Warner Company

Photo credits: Front cover-Courtesy of NASA. 1-P. Jude/Science Photo Library. 20-A. Hart-Davis/Science Photo Library; J. Mead/Science Photo Library. 21-M. Reed/ Eye Ubiquitous. 23-R. Folwell/Science Photo Library. 25-T. Craddock/Science Photo Library. 27-S. Miller/Eye Ubiquitous; W. Carlson/FLPA Ltd. 47-NASA/Science Photo Library. 79-P. Plailly/Science Photo Library. Pacific Press Service; Nature Production, Orion Press; Flat Glass Association of Japan; Furuno Electric Co. Ltd